Tearing the Veil

Tearing the Veil
Essays on femininity

Edited by
SUSAN LIPSHITZ

ROUTLEDGE & KEGAN PAUL
London, Henley and Boston

First published in 1978
by Routledge & Kegan Paul Ltd
39 Store Street,
London WC1E 7DD,
Broadway House,
Newtown Road,
Henley-on-Thames,
Oxon RG9 1EN and
9 Park Street,
Boston, Mass. 02108, USA
Printed by Thomson Litho Ltd,
East Kilbride, Scotland
© Routledge & Kegan Paul Ltd 1978

British Library Cataloguing in Publication Data

Tearing the veil.
1. Women - Social conditions
I. Lipshitz, Susan
301.41'2   HQ1206   77-30323

ISBN 0-7100-8721-7

VOILE, VELUM used in the distinction between female clothing and the male toga.

In Hindu writing the veil of Maya conceals the illusion to which this whole world is due, one of entrenched selfhood.

The Romans associated Maia with the Earth Goddess, a word that became Mamma.

Contents

Notes on Contributors

KATHERINE ARNOLD studied anthropology at Durham University and has worked in Ireland and done fieldwork in Peru. Her interest is in the relationship between anthropology and psychoanalysis. She is married and lives in Highgate, and is at present training in psychotherapy.

DANA BREEN was born in the USA and brought up in France and Switzerland. The research she carried out for her doctoral thesis and subsequent book centred around psychological changes in women with the birth of a first child. Dana Breen works as a psychotherapist. Her interests are in psychoanalysis and the psychobiological aspects of femininity.

MARY JACOBUS teaches at Oxford, where she is a fellow of Lady Margaret Hall. She has written a book on Wordsworth, 'Tradition and Experiment in Wordsworth's Lyrical Ballads' (Oxford, 1976), as well as articles and essays on Wordsworth and Hardy, and is at present working on a book about Thomas Hardy and the magazines. She has taught courses on women and fiction at Oxford and in America.

SUSAN LIPSHITZ was born in South Africa but has lived in England for sixteen years. She studied psychology at the University of Sussex and has worked in research, and as a clinician and a tutor in psychology and women's studies since. She has been active in feminist study groups reading Freud and Lacan, and is particularly interested in working in psychoanalytic theory.

MANDY MERCK was born in the USA. She studied English and Philosophy at Smith College, Massachusetts, and read English at St Hugh's College, Oxford. She has worked as a researcher in history and prehistory for several English publishers and as a freelance journalist. At present she is a member of the 'Red Rag' journal collective and works for the London magazine 'Time Out'.

BARBARA TAYLOR is a Canadian who has lived in England for five years. She is currently active in a feminist historians' group in London and is a member of the 'Red Rag' journal collective. Her

article is drawn from her research for her doctoral thesis regis-
tered at the University of Sussex entitled 'The Feminist Theory
and Practice of the Owenite Socialist Movement'.

Introduction

Susan Lipshitz

The essays in this book written by women are about femininity within
patriarchal culture. The work was begun disparately by the individual writers who have a common concern with constructing a
feminist approach to their work and an interest in interpreting
their material in relation to the construction of sex difference.
They were all asked to write within the framework offered by this
book which splits up the apparent conceptual unity of 'femininity'
into the Mother, the Witch, the Whore, the Pure Woman, the Amazon
and the Free Woman. Femininity is explored by the successive
analyses of familiar and conventional notions that link femininity
to illness, weakness, passivity, and an ambiguously valued sexuality.

Since the essays approach each element through the material of a
different discipline - history, anthropology, psychoanalysis and
literature - they do not form a unitary theory of femininity, a
project which remains problematic. However we do attempt an analysis of the construction of femininity at the level of the psychic
and the unconscious, exploring the possibilities of a particular
kind of symbolic interpretation. Whereas anthropologists can be
said to assume as givens both the universality of patriarchy, and
the fact that all their material refers to the problem of women and
their cultural and social containment, this is not true of other
disciplines and theories. Thus this work makes the patriarchal
order the context for an interpretation of the construction of sex
difference and its relation to the reproductive process. We postulate a psychic level of analysis distinct from the level of social
relations at which most symbolic interpretations are made. Often
this is explicitly informed by psychoanalytic theory, giving a
particular force to our symbolic language and to the unconscious
meanings that we infer. In my introduction to each essay I empha-
sise this connection. However, it should be said that not all the
writers began their work with a particularly Freudian orientation.
Nor is that theory necessarily their central concern. We have
raised a number of questions which are unanswerable here, about the
relationship between these disciplines, about whether it is legitimate to use rituals, myths, polemics and art as texts for psychoanalytic or another type of symbolic interpretation, and about language
and the reading of history.

The consistency of the essays lies in their methodological
approach, for all work with the assumption that femininity is a
meaning that is constructed and relates the feminine subject to
representations of her conditions of existence and to the female
body. We see the patriarchal order not only as a system of power
relations but as a system of meanings in which maleness is standard
and certain elements of femininity, notably its association with
strength or homosexuality, are excluded. The recurrence throughout
the book of the themes of possession, illness, a good and bad mother
image, women described as aliens and outsiders, and the celebration
or subjugation of female sexuality, might be seen as evidence for a
natural and inevitable result of biological sex differences reflected at a psychological level. However, what emerges is rather the
suggestion of a very subtle process of definition that insists on
particular ways of being and perceiving as natural which can be
interpreted as acquired. There is an indication of a consistent
cultural construction of femininity for both men and women that we
see referred to and constructed by certain practices - childbirth,
prostitution, possession, literature, history and feminist politics - discussed in the book. Each element of femininity as expressed in the cultural stereotype is then examined as an ideological element independent of biological and economic factors. It was
this psychic level of analysis that Freud argued ought to be recognised when he wrote

> It seems likely that what are known as materialist views of
> history sin in underestimating this factor. They brush it aside
> with the remark that human 'ideologies' are nothing other than
> the product and superstructure of their contemporary economic
> conditions. This is true, but very probably not the whole truth.
> Mankind never lives entirely in the present. The past, the tra-
> dition of the race and of the people, lives on in the ideologies
> of the superego, and yields only slowly to the influence of the
> present and to new changes; and so long as it operates through
> the superego it plays a powerful part in human life, independent-
> ly of economic conditions. (Freud, 1933, 'Dissection of the
> Personality')

With its formulation of a structured unconscious and of fantasy and
its recognition of an always sexed self, Freudian theory can contribute to our analysis of the persistence of the organisation of
female sexuality and psychological sex difference. As these essays
show, sanctions against the expression of female sexuality for
'pleasure' rather than for reproduction occur at the levels of
fantasy and the unconscious as well as in the social organisation
of legitimate inheritance through the family, law, the State, etc.
Although the essays vary in their approach to the problem of female
sexuality, the structuring of this split constantly re-emerges in
their material, for example, in the essays of the first section on
the Mother, the Witch, and the Whore. Freudian theory can contribute to our understanding of the significance of such a
structuring, but, as I suggested earlier, there are problems in
appropriating it; since the theory itself is neither simple nor
consistent, difficulties created by its application are compounded.
Furthermore the material being interpreted has not arisen in the
psychoanalytic treatment situation. The varying degrees of success

of these essays and the speculative nature of their interpretation
depends partly on the slippage found in the theory itself between
the autonomous psychic level postulated, and its reduction at times
to biology or the level of social relations. In the historical
essays on the Amazon and the Free Woman there is a similar difficulty in maintaining a particular definition of ideology and at the
same time constructing it in relation to particular case material.
This work, then, is 'in progress', but we hope it will encourage
other work in this area by its making comprehensible in different
ways the construction of the feminine within patriarchy.

Psychoanalytic theory offers us ways of analysing ideological
processes in terms of the construction of individual subjectivity
as a psychic force. The individual is always a sexed subject in
that there is always a place in culture and in a family for a boy
or girl child before they are born. Yet, simultaneously, there is
some doubt about how the subject will locate him or her self. According to Freud (and other psychoanalytic writers) this process is
related to the child successfully developing autonomy from the
mother, who is at first the child's whole world and from whom it is
undifferentiated. (The essay on the Mother explores her feelings
about the process, and throughout the book there is an emphasis on
women's own expression of their experience as the raw material of
our interpretation.) Additionally, the cultural demand is that the
child's sexuality, which is inextricable from its self, favours
genitality in the interest of reproduction. Bisexuality and the
component instincts of looking, touching and hurting have to be
bound together in particular form. Some feminists have rejected
Freudian theory not only because, read in this way, it can seem
biologically determinist, and not only because it is written out
fully for males and implies only that female development is 'the
opposite'. There is also a difficulty in challenging the theory,
and in deciding on its precise relationship to the theoretical
concerns of feminists. A particular problem is the apparent
equation of narcissism and femininity, femininity and illness,
antisocial interest and thus immorality, insatiability and lack of
self-control - in brief the description of women as forces of nature
and not culture.

It is the Oedipus crisis that classically institutionalises this
cultural control and leads to the formation of the superego which is
mentioned in the previous quotation from Freud. It is in the
difference between males and females psychologically, in their
morality and in their internal conscience that is the superego, that
the inferiority of the feminine is said to consist. The following
account schematises Freud's theory of the castration complex, a
fantasy produced by the child who is attempting to deal with the
problem of sex difference, and one that determines the effectiveness
of the structuring of gender at the Oedipal moment. However, it
will help the reader to grasp how this characterisation of women,
said to associate them with wild nature, can actually be read
instead as an analysis of the process of the structuring of femininity and female sexuality and the construction of feminine images.
This schematic account is specifically given here so that it can
serve to locate those essays in this book which use psychoanalytic
theory explicitly in their work, as in the first part, as well as

serving as a background for those of the second part where reference
is made to the unconscious, to theories of sex difference embodied
in religious and political and moral ideologies and where, implicitly, the definition of ideology invokes such levels of analysis.
This section raises large questions about the relation of social to
psychic forces and the relation between theories of history, literature and social change. The focus of the book as a whole, however,
is the psychic level and our interest is to pose questions about sex
difference within culture in such a way as to make the phallo-
centrism of this culture visible.

At the Oedipal moment the child has to locate itself as a masculine or feminine subject by taking on an identification with the
appropriate sex parent. Both girls and boys have to give up their
mother as love object and the person with whom they first identified. The little boy has to learn to choose a woman other than his
mother to love and later have children by. He debates in accordance
with his bisexuality whether to take his mother's place in relation
to his father, i.e. to be passive, or whether to accept his active,
masculine place. The felt threat of castration from his father
usually effectively structures the boy's choice of the latter position. Once he abandons incestuous desire he accepts the father's
authority (as possessor of the mother) and the patriarchal cultural
order. The repression of the boy's desire for his mother leads to
the formation of the boy's superego in its place. Now since the
girl in this theory is already castrated, her repression and thus
the formation of her superego are said to be less effective. She
is said to remain more narcissistic than the boy whose own first
love of his mother and his image of himself are more firmly abandon-
ed. That is to say, the boy's narcissism is left behind in two
ways. Through the process of the structuring of psychological sex
difference, and as part of the abandonment of an infantile belief in
his own and his mother's perfection and wholeness, the child sepa-
rates and develops a self. (The importance of the pre-Oedipal phase
has been elaborated by post-Freudian analysts, notably by Klein.
There is only space here to note this and to point out that several
of the book's essays refer to the child's earlier fantasies, particularly to the split between the good and bad mother image, examining its implications for a healthy female self-concept.) What
is often overlooked is the fact that children of both sexes go
through the phases described. And perhaps at this point we glimpse
the impact of ideological accounts of the origin not only of Man and
Nature, but as the essays on the Amazon and the Free Woman show
clearly, that of Man and Woman which are made equivalent to Man and
Nature, reinforcing a split at the social level between those with
and without social and economic and political power.

One of the persistent associations with 'femininity' is narcissism, and this has been taken by some feminists to imply that
women are then necessarily lost in imaginary realms, ill, and inac-
cessibly in love with their own image. These are other ways in
which they are supposedly 'natural' and located outside of a culture
they cannot enter. I suggest instead that, given that women have
language, morality and cultural categories in common with men, they
do enter culture, but in a different way. Their position is one
that refers them always to their not-maleness, their relation to the

castration complex structuring their entry so that they always have to make sense of that lack. Women face a double lack; both the absence of the phallus and the lack of wholeness which every child constantly attempts to recognise. Ideology represents the subject to itself as whole, and this has a particular meaning for women since the wholeness of our notion of femininity is shown here to have particular contradictions.

Psychoanalytic theory helps to clarify how the meaning of sexual difference denied by repression, disavowal or censorship, structures the location of women. In various ways these essays document their displacement from a central position in cultural categories and their rendering socially powerless or irresponsible in politics as in art. We try to show how women are thus constructed in ideology and explore some of the ambivalent feelings that this arouses in men and women themselves.

THE MOTHER

This aspect of femininity is central to any analysis of female psychology, and has a variety of possible forms. The approach chosen for this essay develops a discussion of the impact of pregnancy and childbirth on the mother at the level of fantasy, and suggests ways in which these are articulated with certain medical practices. While practices like induction, removal of the newborn child from its mother to a nursery, or the use of pain-killers during childbirth, can save the mother pain or even damage, they can also effectively structure her maternity so that she feels helpless, passive and violated.

The reported fantasies and experiences of women are related to the unconscious meaning they reveal of a woman's maternity to her-self and others. Pregnancy which signifies impending maternity arouses childhood impressions and theories about where babies come from, mixed feelings and anxieties about repeating the woman's own mother's pattern of care or neglect, and about the woman's feminity. The crisis may be one where the ambivalence aroused and felt to be in conflict with the ideal of maternity as woman's natural destiny and crowning achievement remains unresolved. Medical practices that reinforce the inevitable insecurities of this time may not only preempt a resolution but may aid the disavowal or denial of the conflicts. This in turn can increase the chances of mental disturbance after childbirth. It is suggested that women need to resolve the split between an unconscious image of a good and bad mother and to identify themselves with the former. In doing so they recognise their own adult sexuality and rather than this being a passive resignation, the most competent mothers studied here were shown to associate maternity with activity.

> Even in the sphere of human sexual life you soon see how inade-
> quate it is to make masculine behaviour coincide with activity
> and feminine with passivity. A mother is active in every sense
> towards her child; the act of lactation itself may equally be
> described as the mother suckling the baby or as her being sucked
> by it. (Freud, 1933, 'Femininity')

Such activity is vital for a woman's self-image, for her relation-

ship to her child and to men. Instead of her being seen as ill and
weak because of her body, or functionally masochistic because of the
pain she endures, this meaning of pregnancy and childbirth trans-
forms the possible meaning of femininity. There is a recognition
that the woman's own childhood experiences as well as her adult ones
will affect her maternity and that these effects are not expected to
be entirely conscious. This makes possible an analysis of the
cultural medical rituals in particular that mediate the change from
childless woman into mother as constructing a particular version of
the maternal identity which has an inflection making a positive
resolution hard or even impossible. And this is in spite of the
apparent cultural idealisation and valuation of a woman's capacity
to give birth and the expectation that she will be able, all un-
tutored, to nurture a child.

THE WITCH

The association of femininity and illness as a function of the
limitation of psychical female sexuality for reproduction is
discussed here. Women can be thought of as witch-like in having
the power to create live beings, a capacity that could be thought
to be part of their mystery. However, women's accusation and
persecution as witches in history or in other cultures seems to
be explicable as a social process and in terms of social relations.
Their 'reality' is not in doubt since the women were convinced of
their power to harm and so were the communities in which they lived.
   However, it is the psychic conditions that make for the meaning
of the bewitching and the possession or illness of women that are
examined here. The difference between these types of analysis is
exemplified by this observation; if illness at menopause could
be abolished by giving women compensatory political power at a
time when they can no longer produce children nor need to devote
their time to child-care, then women's oppression could be allevi-
ated by rational means. Since this is not the case, the persistence
of particular associations of femininity and masculinity respectively with illness and health, have to be understood in the context of
the construction of male and female relations within culture and
in the unconscious. The constraint of cultural femininity by the
heterosexual imperative also sets up a double-bind in which to be
feminine is not to be adult and thus not to be healthy because the
standard for these characteristics is a male one. This essay
demonstrates the use of Freudian theory which recognises the
symbolism of female illness as a language of sexuality and sees
symptoms as speaking of its limitation in the construction of the
feminine.

THE WHORE

This examination of the relationship between femininity and sexual
insatiability takes as its focus a Peruvian brothel. The prostitute's relationship to her client is interpreted symbolically and in
the context of the machismo ideology of Peruvian culture. The eco-

nomic aspect of prostitution takes second place because we consider
that a serious psychological study of the bases of prostitution
should be continued, possibly using the work of Geza Roheim as a
starting place. To see prostitution simply as work whose conditions
need bettering is to ignore the psychological forces that account
for the prostitute's continued existence. Apart from Kate Millett's
interviews with several American prostitutes and serious surveys
like William Acton's of the nineteenth-century brothel-based English
prostitution, there is a tendency for any work that takes the
psychological aspects of prostitution into account to be voyeuristic
and titillating. In this it is often not far from feeding the same
appetites it seems to condemn in the men who use prostitutes and in
those who read about them.

This study of a brothel as a social institution suggests that its
rituals articulate with unconscious and ambivalent ideas and
feelings about women. They are either the Madonna or the Whore, a
split described by Freud in his essays on love and a dual image
which develops in the context of the child's relation to its mother.
For she is both the good provider of satisfaction and yet is discovered to be separate and sexual in relating to the father. Such
currents of fantasy, in which one woman is worthy of love and another is sexual and to be degraded, form romantic love's images.
They persist into adulthood and seem to be part of the activities
of this brothel. The men both need the prostitutes and yet fear and
degrade them. So do their respectable wives. For the morality of
the conventional Peruvian marriage seems complemented by the place
of the prostitute. She is feared and hemmed in by health rules and
regulations and is literally placed on the outskirts of town. But
she is also accepted as having a place. Sex for pleasure and sex
for reproduction are clearly split between the home and the brothel.
What this means to both respectable and disreputable women is con-
veyed, in particular the prostitute's own awareness of her use as a
receptacle for the bad aspects of sexuality.

In describing the relationships between male client and female
prostitute as reminiscent of that between mother and child, we are
not saying they are the same. But the power of such an interpretation is its having made comprehensible what were hitherto considered merely perverse and invisible activities. How far this
analysis applies to the different situation of individual women
controlled by pimps or operating alone in illegal, covert activities, remains to be explored both in the Peruvian context and in
other societies.

THE PURE WOMAN

An author, we hear people say, should keep out of the way of any
contact with psychiatry and should leave the description of
pathological mental states to the doctors. The truth is that no
truly creative writer has ever obeyed this injunction. The description of the human mind is indeed the domain which is most
his own: he has from time immemorial been the precursor of
science, and so too of scientific psychology. But the frontier
between states of mind described as normal and pathological is

in part a conventional one and in part so fluctuating that each
of us probably crosses it many times in the course of a day.
(Freud, 1906, 'Jensen's Gradiva')

Thomas Hardy's creation of Tess in 'Tess of the d'Urbervilles' in
1891 was demonstrably affected by the censorship of the critics of
the age. The bargaining between author and publishers and the
reaction of the critics concerned the permissible portrait of a
woman. While the controversy appears as a debate between individuals with different moralities, the documentation also shows precisely what linguistic and behavioural rules were to be obeyed in
the portrayal of Tess's sexuality and the extent of her responsibility for her fall. The creation of an acceptably 'pure' femininity was accomplished by Hardy's cleansing of her image. In the
early versions of the story a more sexually aware woman brought
about her own condition, whereas in the final draft she is rather a
victim of circumstances and male privilege – the subject of a
polemic in which she must appear more sinned against than sinning.
This process is effected by minor word changes as well as variations
in the novel's plot, and called for a revision of the male characters as well as of Tess. To impose a psychoanalytic interpretation
of the novel, unstated by Hardy, may be illegitimate. But the power
of the novel lies partly in its exploration of the dynamics of romantic and sexual love and its tension with the character's own
desire, unrecognised by them all and yet at times indicated by the
power of unconscious forces erupting in the story. Tess, Alec and
Angel all recognise the right of her first seducer over her, a
sexual thraldom that can only be broken by Alec's murder. This
violation of the law at both the social and symbolic levels has to
be punished. In Tess's journeys through the valleys of life and
death in the farms she works on, she is apparently gaining courage
and desperation to destroy this bondage. In a moment of passion or
madness she does so, with entirely comprehensible pleasure. This
authenticity is largely lost with the purification of Tess, but
enough has been recovered of the original text to indicate here the
power of its theme and perhaps the reasons for its censorship –
Hardy's unconstrained presentation of Tess's passionate sexuality.

THE AMAZON

The Greek city's achievement of the title, it is argued here, is its
use of the mythic Amazon as a trophy of conquest. Contrary to the
pervasive mythology of Amazons as warrior women who were part of a
lost golden age when women ruled the world in an essentially benign
feminine way, this essay argues that they were an ideological construction. The claim is carefully documented first with contemporary accounts of the real and legendary wars between the Greeks and
their foreign foes, and then with reference to the social and economic place of women in ancient Greece. The various guises in which
Amazons appear in Greek histories, vase paintings and murals as the
enemy, an enemy of male heroes whose feats ensured the continuity of
Greek civilisation and the maintenance of social order, demonstrates
the flexibility of the image and argues for its construction in the
interests of patriotism.

Such a reading of the Amazon is not usual; nineteenth-century writers like Bachofen postulated a matriarchal stage in their fashionably evolutionist account of the history of culture. This stage was said to be a precursor of patriarchy, and a more primitive and less moral order. Bachofen also saw this era as one of greater altruism and dominated by warm, caring, earth-bound power as opposed to the later necessarily more scientific and yet hard, masculine era. 'Matriarchal existence is regulated naturalism,' he said, 'its thinking, material, its development predominantly physical. Mother-right is just as essential to this cultural stage as it is alien and unintelligible to the era of patriarchy.' According to him the Amazons were a group of women protesting at their abuse in group marriage situations and a part of the movement that persuaded indi-vidual men to take pride in their own offspring, thus enforcing their responsibility for the children through the institutional-isation of monogamy. Amazonism is said to be preparation for a stage of conjugal motherhood and part of a universal cultural pro-gression from a material to a spiritual age. The same progression was described in universalistic psychic terms by Jungians like Briffault and Neumann. It is these sources that are mostly uncriti-cally drawn on by later writers like Diner and Davis, who describe their aim as the recovery of the female heritage and the history of female power. They in turn are followed by some contemporary femi-nist writings. In this discussion of the Amazon in a particular historical period, related to the particular conditions of Athenian economy and society, the image can be seen as mythic. This inevita-bly raises questions about the Victorian myth of the Amazon which needs to be similarly examined in its specificity. The inevitabili-ty of the conquest of the strong woman is unresolved. What is suggested here is that, at least in such heroic form, the associ-ation of femininity with strength is not part of the accepted cultural meaning of femininity.

THE FREE WOMAN

Woman-power describes the relationship of nineteenth-century femi-nist ideology to chiliastic religious doctrines, and in particular to the preachings of Joanna Southcott. In this discussion of the association of femininity with forms of political power usually dismissed as marginal to working-class struggle, we see how the women of the early radical movements were able to use the language of heresy to challenge many of the elements of the concept of femi-ninity discussed in the other essays. The language of the polemics was that of religion and the forum of struggle was the Owenite socialist and labour organisations.

From the point of view of this book, what is striking is how a political challenge, launched with anti-clerical impetus, seemed necessarily to involve an ideological struggle that directed at-tention to the myths of evil female sexuality and feminine weakness, used in the refusal of women's rights to power. In the Southcottian doctrines, the Godhead is transformed into a woman or at least an androgynous being, which can be seen as an attempt to reverse the cultural mythology that was felt to be part of the power of patri-

archal society. Engels greatly admired the Owenites as a movement
not afraid of the facts, even when they clashed with the book of
Genesis. In order to 'find people who dared use their own intellectual faculties with regard to religious matters, you had to go
amongst the uneducated, the "great unwashed" as they were called,
the working people especially the Owenite Socialists' (Engels,
'Historical Materialism'). In this the strength of the Owenite
women is recognised, as they were unafraid to challenge the religious dogmas that sustained male supremacy and recognised the
misogynism of so much Christian theology. This necessary challenge
to the Church and its doctrines led to Owenism becoming a platform
for feminist heresy. Their own church, the Communist Church, did
include in its writings an attempt to define a new morality. For
example, the moral force of feminine nature was urged and there were
hopes that it would be integrated with the male principle in the establishment of a new order of love and charity.

The political and psychological levels cannot be conflated: the
desire or lack of the feminine subject outlined earlier is not the
cause of the search for La Mère, for instance. Women were not
simply seeking the pre-Oedipal mother. For to reduce history to
psychological mechanisms is to deny the specificity of levels of
analysis. Only when theory is more developed can we hope to articulate the relationships between them. What we do have here is a
unique account of the interpenetration of psychological, economic,
social and political forces in the development of the feminist
movement of the last century which has resonances in our present
Women's Liberation Movement. Not least, the similarity lies in
their posing the question of female sexuality and femininity as ones
that will not of themselves be resolved, even if there were revolutionary political change, thus facing us with the question of
their construction within ideology.

Finally, as the editor of this book I should like to thank all the
contributors who made it interesting. They cannot, of course, be
held responsible for flaws in its conception.

ACKNOWLEDGMENTS

The editor and publishers are grateful to the following for per-
mission to quote from the works cited, in the Introduction and in
Chapter 2: Sigmund Freud Copyrights Ltd, The Institute of Psycho-
Analysis and The Hogarth Press for 'the Standard Edition of the
Complete Psychological Works of Sigmund Freud', revised and edited
by James Strachey; W.W.Norton & Company Inc. for 'New Introductory
Lectures' by Sigmund Freud; George Allen & Unwin Ltd for 'Intro-
ductory Lectures on Psychoanalysis' by Sigmund Freud; Basic Books
Inc. for 'Studies in Hysteria' by Sigmund Freud and Josef Breuer.

SELECTED BIBLIOGRAPHY

ALTHUSSER, L., 'Lenin and Philosophy', New Left Books, 1971.
BACHOFEN, J.J., 'Myth, Religion and Motherright', Princeton
University Press edition, 1967.
DAVIS, E.G., 'The First Sex', Penguin, 1972.
DOUGLAS, M., 'Witchcraft, Confessions and Accusations', Tavistock,
1970.
ENGELS, F., 'The Origin of the Family, Private Property and the
State', International Publishers edition, 1970.
ENGELS, F., 'Historical Materialism', Pluto Press edition, 1971.
FREUD, S., 'Three Essays on the Theory of Sexuality', 1905;
Complete Psychological Works of Sigmund Freud, Standard Edition,
vol.7, Hogarth Press and the Institute of Psychoanalysis.
FREUD, S., 'Jensen's Gradiva', 1906; Complete Works, vol.9.
FREUD, S., 'Contribution to the Psychology of Love', Complete Works,
vol.11.
FREUD, S., 'On Narcissism', Complete Works, vol.14.
FREUD, S., 'New Introductory Lectures', Complete Works, vol.22.
HARDY, T., 'Tess of the d'Urbervilles', Macmillan, 1965.
KRISTEVA, J., 'Des Chinoises', Editions des Femmes, 1974.
LACAN, J., 'Ecrits', Editions du Seuil, Paris, 1966.
LA FONTAINE, J. (ed.), 'The Interpretation of Ritual', Tavistock,
1972.
LAPLANCHE, J. and PONTALIS, J-B., 'The Language of Psycho-analysis',
Hogarth Press, 1973.
LEVI-STRAUSS, C., 'Structural Anthropology', Allen Lane, the Penguin
Press, 1968.
LEWIS, I., 'Ecstatic Religion', Penguin, 1971.
MEPHAM, J., 'The Theory of Ideology in Capital', Radical Philosophy,
1970.
MILLETT, K., 'The Prostitution Papers', Paladin, 1975.
MITCHELL, J., 'Psychoanalysis and Feminism', Allen Lane, 1974.

Part one

Sexuality and the Body

THE MOTHER

Motherhood is integral to the pervasive idea of femininity, and the female capacity to reproduce children is both an envied and denigrated part of womanhood. Present practices surrounding childbirth in hospitals and postnatal practices around breast feeding make it extremely difficult for women to make the birth of a child into a positive experience, a process of growth, a new discovery of primitive feelings and the beginning of a spontaneous relationship with their baby.

Chapter 1

The Mother and the Hospital

An unfortunate fit between the
woman's internal world and some
hospital practices

Dana Breen

ACKNOWLEDGMENTS

With thanks to Dr Jenny Lewis, Ian Birksted, Stuart Marks and
Dr Abe Brafman for their constructive criticism.

Pregnancy, and in particular a first pregnancy, is a bio-psycho-
social event involving the woman's sexuality, which requires coming
to terms with past relationships, mourning the 'old-self', working
through fears and fantasies about the birth and the new baby, making
room for a new person, coming to terms with a new life style, coming
to grips with a realistic notion of the 'good enough mother'. (1)
    This paper is an attempt to describe how external structures (in
this case certain hospital practices) can articulate with these internal psychological conflicts, thereby increasing the chances of
pathological reactions around the time of childbirth.
    I will start by describing the psychological processes of change
and the conflicts which take place in women at the time of having a
baby, contrasting women who cope well with those who do not cope so
well.
    I will then go on, in the second section, to look at the way in
which some characteristics of the institutional setting come to slot
in with certain anxieties and with less adaptive ways of dealing
with the feelings aroused at the time of having a baby.

I CONFLICT AND GROWTH

Pregnancy has often been described implicitly or explicitly as a
hurdle which must be overcome in order for the woman to get back to
her normal pre-pregnancy state, or an illness from which she must
and in most cases does recover. As one pamphlet for expectant
fathers puts it: 'you will find that the middle months of pregnancy
are a more stable period and "normality" returns some weeks after
the baby's birth' (my emphasis). (2) This abnormality which colours
the pregnant period is ascribed to bodily processes. In the words

of another pamphlet: 'the probable reason lies in the complex
series of chemical changes that are taking place throughout the
body and in particular in the placenta (or after-birth).' (3)   The
woman is told not to worry because these strange emotions are not
a part of her but are an artifact of the physiological changes and
will disappear when she regains her former figure.   Husbands are
told to be patient and to remember that their wife is not really
the way she is at the moment, that she is temporarily 'possessed'.
Psychological studies are also frequently based on this notion of
a temporary disorder and women are tested for evidence of increased
'neuroticism' during pregnancy with an expectation that their scores
will return to pre-pregnancy measures postnatally. (4)

Such notions of pregnancy as temporary possession by psycho-
chemical forces, as temporary derangement which must be brushed
aside, as illness from which the woman must and will recover, are
not only patronisingly dismissive of what could be a most valued
and specifically female experience, but also deny the importance
and meaningfulness of the turbulent emotions which accompany all
important life events.   Pregnancy stimulates in the woman ideas of
life and death, mortality and immortality, purposefulness and futility, ideas connected with her own infancy, mothering and
fathering, about her own ability to nurture and be relied upon,
about dependency, about her own capacity to be intimately and bodily
involved with a newborn baby and later a child while at the same
time able to retain a sense of individuality.   These questions may
not necessarily be so clearly formulated, but they cannot but be
experienced in some form by a woman preparing to give birth to a
child, and the turbulent and sometimes incomprehensible emotions
relate in one way or another to these sorts of questions.   In fact
one can talk about a 'capacity to worry' in the face of such a major
life event.   To worry is also to prepare oneself for the change
which will take place and it is the woman who has no anxieties at
all during pregnancy who is likely to experience psychological
difficulties after the birth of the baby.   To talk about temporary
derangement or 'increased neuroticism' is not only to misunderstand
this healthy side of being able to worry and come to grips with
mixed feelings and perhaps irrational feelings in the face of a
dramatic event, but is also to deny the personal enrichment a person
can find in coming into touch with the powerful emotions stimulated
by this event, and the meaningfulness of these emotions.   I find it
more appropriate to think of pregnancy as one part of a total
process, pregnancy in a psychological sense of growth and preparation, as a phase of development which can be coped with well or
not so well, depending on various psycho-social aspects and circumstances.   In this sense it is not possible to talk about one particular cut-off point, such as the birth, for instance.   Major
changes and experiences also take place after the birth of the baby,
when reality comes to articulate with fantasy.   I prefer to talk
loosely about 'changes with the birth of a child' - where particular
feelings or the resolution of certain conflicts can take place at
different points and at a different pace for each particular woman.

Instead of getting stuck on specific symptoms (nausea, tiredness,
etc.) accompanying the psychophysiological process of pregnancy and
which are akin to those of certain illnesses (and can feel with no

doubt most debilitating), it is more fruitful to look at the meaning
of the total process for a woman. The birth of a child and in particular a first child is a meaningful experience which cannot leave
a woman unaffected. If she is able to integrate this experience and
change, one can talk of 'growth' and 'development'. In the words of
Abigail Lewis, for whom it is a question of femininity versus masculinity:

> the defiant tomboy that was me will be finally and irrevocably
> lost, but 'someone else will be born', though not so apparently
> as the baby is born. Or at least I hope so... 'one must learn
> to change with changing circumstances or it is death indeed'. (5)
> (Emphasis mine.)

A woman during pregnancy often comes closer to her childhood
feelings, to reconsidering her past. She questions her position and
her role.

> Living far from home, in a separate life, I have come to feel at
> times in charge of my destiny, free of my blood. But certain
> doubts leak through. I have been a daughter, I shall be a
> mother. But what is there between? Am I anchored to this line
> forever? (Hermine Demoriane) (6)

That she has had a mother and that she will be a mother are ines-
capable facts. But what does this mean exactly to each woman, what
does it mean in terms of what she feels about her mother, about
motherhood and about her ability to mother? What does it mean in
terms of the constraints she feels it places on her person? And
beyond this what does it mean in terms of being a woman able to bear
children? For Hermine Demoriane being thrown in this way back into
her past seems to mean a certain loss of freedom, and her feelings
concerning her own dependency are acutely aroused.

I found (7) that it is possible to describe processes of change
in women with the birth of a first child. The focus in my study was
on the changes in how women see themselves and their perception of
the maternal role. I compared a group of women who coped well with
having a baby (from both a psychological and a somatic point of
view) with a group of women who did not cope well. Indeed opposite
processes of change took place in these two groups of women. For
the women who coped well (in the sense of psychological and physiological well-being) the processes included an identification with a
good mother image, a reconsideration of the mother role which they
could feel in tune with, a resolution when necessary of the split
between 'goddess' and 'witch'. This split in the image of the
mother is one which psychoanalysts locate in the earliest experience
of the infant who does not yet connect the experience of contentment
of one moment with the rage of another, and creates separate images
of destruction and goodness. How these images are later integrated
and the balance between them, will depend on the particular child
and the woman's life circumstances. Specific events reawaken the
fear of this destructive force inside or outside the person, or the
hope for a source of total satisfaction. At the time of having a
baby these images of the perfect mother and the totally bad mother
are reactivated through the woman becoming a mother herself, and
becoming the mother to a newborn baby coming from herself and like
she once was. The mother who copes, I found, is the one who is able
to come to terms with her own past, find in herself a positive

mother image, neither idealised nor denigrated, which she can call
upon and identify with in relation to the new baby. I found that
one of the things which makes this possible is that her standards
are not pitched too high; to be a good mother, she comes to realise, is in large part a question of hard work and she is able to
meet this demand to a reasonable extent. What happens to the non-
coping mother is quite different. After the birth of the baby, even
more than before, she sets unrealistically high standards for herself. The good mother she sees as one who is perfect and totally
self-sacrificing. This is the mother she feels she never had and
also the one she feels she cannot possibly be. She feels inadequate
and bad. Against this background the baby's cries and demands are
felt as accusations and proofs of her inadequacy. She feels angry
or guilty and thinks her badness is confirmed. For this woman, the
internal split between the ideal mother and the terrible one, far
from being resolved is increased, the childhood split between
goddess and witch predominates. How a woman sees the maternal role
in terms of the rest of her life is also important. I found in my
study that the coping women were either satisfied by and identified
with a very traditionally defined role after the birth of the baby,
or on the contrary were able to recreate the mother role in such a
way that they could positively identify with it without finding it
too restricting. The non-coping women tended to perceive the mother
role in a more traditionally idealised way after the birth of the
baby, and this involved for them a greater conflict with outside
interests and a greater dichotomy between what they wanted to do
and what they felt they ought to do.

There are many reasons why one woman can reconsider the maternal
role and be satisfied with herself as a mother while another woman
suffers at not being the selfless mother she feels she ought to be.
The role played by the institutional setting will be considered in
the second section of this paper. Psychological factors stemming
from her own early life will colour her aspirations and perception
of herself as a mother in the way I described earlier. The behaviour of the particular baby will also be important in either
helping a woman feel at peace with herself or on the contrary confirming her feeling of inadequacy. One woman describes this in relation to her two children:

John cried and cried and cried and he used to wake all the other
babies up (in hospital), as soon as he'd open his eyes he cried,
at night all the babies would wake up and be fed and he'd scream,
every night I had to go to the nursery and every night they had
to give me a sleeping tablet because I got in such a state....
I felt very rejected because he cried all the time and in the end
very resentful, rejected by him, I never seemed to be able to do
anything right.... Jane is so placid. John would open his eyes
and scream, Jane would think about it before she let rip and even
when she did it wasn't this terrible pitch, John used to have
this terrible pitch which used to really jar, hers is rather
apologetic, and she's been fabulous.... She's so loving. Everything I do is right.... I still feel guilty at how angry John
can make me. I don't know how much was the fact that he was a
difficult baby or how much that I was a difficult mother, I
really don't know, or how much I resented him, maybe I just
resented how having him made me feel.

While for this woman it is the placid baby who makes her feel a good mother, for another woman it would be such a placid baby who would arouse the fantasy that he or she could die any minute, or be lacking in healthy vitality.

Psycho-social factors related to a woman's present socio-economic and work situation are also important and determine the extent of the change in circumstances brought about by the pregnancy and the new baby. How much a woman gives up economically, professionally or in terms of independence will vary and colour her feelings about being a mother. And also it may well be easier to feel a loving mother when all the time and energy are not taken up with coping with other children and a house single-handed, and there is no possibility of escaping for a few hours from the constant demands. This is where the actual amount of practical help given by the father of the baby also comes in. For as well as his perception of her as a mother (if he is supportive rather than denigrating of her mothering capacity) he can practically help to make her life less stressful.

One small study of women who had a psychotic breakdown after the birth of the baby suggested that the husbands of these women tended to compete with their wives in the female role, thus contributing further to the wives' feelings of inadequacy. The authors talk about these men as being the counterpart to what has been described as 'castrating women'. (8) The man's own early images of the ideal-ised and the denigrated mother, and his definition of the mother role will have an effect on the marital relationship and the woman's feelings about herself as a mother.

Besides the ability to reconsider the maternal role so as to be in tune with a not too idealised image of it, the women who in my study coped well were able to feel themselves to be active and cre-ative during pregnancy. After the birth of the baby the sense of activity of the coping women and the sense of passivity of the non-coping women were in even greater contrast. This is strikingly different from the traditional equation of femininity with passivi-ty, since it is here possible to show that a good adjustment to this uniquely female experience goes with a feeling of initiation and activity. The evident activity necessary in childbirth itself has been referred to as masculine. One author talks of the 'masculine achievement of giving birth'. (9) I think this is absurd. The qualities necessary for coping with childbearing are by definition feminine, and if such essential qualities are activity and a sense of creativity, then these qualities are an integral part of femi-ninity (in the sense of femaleness).

II   IN HOSPITAL

The birth itself

Childbirth is symbolic of the passage from non-mother to mother. It is the moment from which the primiparous woman (i.e. a woman pregnant for the first time) will be called a mother although she has already nurtured this child for nine months. For the woman who has already borne a child it symbolises the beginning of a new

cycle. Anthropologists have described how other cultures deal with
this momentous event by surrounding it with various practices and
elaborate 'rites de passage'. The psychoanalyst Peter Lomas suggests that similar practices can be described in our own culture, in
particular the seclusion of the parturient woman away from the rest
of the family and from her usual habitat, and the powerful role
which is given to the doctor in relation to the pregnant and parturient woman. (10)

Like other ceremonies, these practices can be symbolically
helpful in regulating the transition, framing it into rigid rules
of behaviour and offering a transition time without pressures. The
week's rest in hospital is supposed to allow the new mother to take
charge of her baby in her own time, under the supervision of the
more experienced 'mothers'. Mistakes are tolerated and she is told
to follow strict procedures and timetables. The whole seclusion in
hospital is one which emphasises and condones the special nature of
the event, its major implications, and allows a period of read-
justment away from the strains of everyday life. It also helps a
woman to feel protected against the strong emotions evoked by
childbirth; she feels in a safe place, well protected by the
doctor. The woman's fears are partly due to her fantasy of the
harm which could incur to herself and the baby and partly based on
the reality of the envy which is stimulated by a parturient woman.
Indeed some of the practices such as that of removing the babies
from their mothers soon after birth can, I think, best be understood
as the result of the unconscious wish to disrupt and disturb the
intimate relationship between mother and baby. I will come back to
this later.

Although these practices carry with them an aspect of reassurance, the other side of the coin is the restrictions they impose.
For the women who can tolerate and enjoy the confusion, novelty and
unpredictability of this exciting event, a hospital confinement can
feel barbaric in its controlled asepsis. Added to this, are the
detrimental effects of the sadistic components of the practices
(such as the separation of mother and baby) and the harm caused by
the 'medicalisation of life' with its emphasis on hygiene and on
people as well or ill functioning machines. The pregnant woman is
told to scrub her nipples, (11) the young mother is told not to have
the baby in her bed because of germs. (12) The woman having a baby
is treated as if her body were ill, needing constant monitoring,
until it finally returns to normality six weeks after the birth of
the baby. Her experience of having a baby is not considered.

The argument given in favour of the medicalisation of labour is
a decrease in morbidity (in particular perinatal mortality) in relation to obstetrical measures. Without entering a debate about
whether the decrease in perinatal mortality is not in fact due
mainly to better ante-natal care rather than obstetrical interventions, it is worth pointing out the distinction between discussion at an abstract level and what actually takes place. For
example, no one would deny the extreme cases which require a cae-
sarian or an induction of labour for the baby to survive, and yet
in another case the same procedure could be harmful to the mother
(in colouring her feelings about herself and the baby) and the baby
(when the baby is born prematurely, for instance). One author cites

'an obstetrician justifying non-medical induction on the grounds
that as it is good for those who already have clinical problems it
must be even better for those who are completely normal.' (13)

And then one must remember that any intervention is liable to
human errors and mismanagement. When I was in labour with my first
child, the midwife insisted that I ingest some pills to speed up
labour. I told her that I thought things were progressing sufficiently quickly. She insisted. I asked her what these pills were
and she replied: 'they're male hormones, we also give them for
abortions.' (An extraordinary statement to make to a woman in
labour.) With the help of my husband we were able to apply to
higher authorities and I was allowed not to take these 'abortive'
pills. The whole of my labour lasted only two and a half hours and
I shudder to think what would have happened to my daughter or to me
had I accepted to have the speed of my labour hastened. (This, by
the way, took place in one of London's foremost teaching hospitals.)

There is a danger in thinking of medical interventions as being
on the whole a nuisance but in any case helpful or at most inef-
fective. One forgets the frequent occurrences in which these interventions, through error, ignorance or carelessness are positively
harmful.

Childbirth is treated as a physiological event and it is often
forgotten that not only does childbirth have a psychological meaning
but, also, that there are psychological aspects involved in the progress of this event.

As an example of this other side of childbirth let us look at
some psychological aspects of the timing of labour (and it is worth
remembering that from the physiological point of view little is
still known about the time of onset of labour). The onset of labour
is experienced differently. Some women want to give birth as soon
as possible while for other women the birth is experienced as a loss
of a part of themselves, or the loss of a treasured possession, and
the approaching date of the birth is experienced with anxiety.
Towards the end of pregnancy a sort of preparation takes place and
the boundary between outside and inside (the pregnant body) becomes
more fluid. Six weeks before my daughter was born I had the following dream: 'for the first time I could grab the baby's arm through
the abdominal wall - I was so excited I called my husband. But then
the baby's hand and nails got stuck in the skin and I panicked
before being able to release it.' Mary, a woman I interviewed,
dreamed that she and her husband took the baby out to have a look at
it, but then they found that they could not put it back in; the
dream was accompanied by a great deal of anxiety and the sense of
punishment for such curiosity. Lesley, another interviewee, wished
that she could keep the baby inside forever, yet at other times she
wondered if the baby was still alive. She dreamed that a dog was
drowning. When she woke up she remembered that the dog was curled
up like a foetus and she realised that she was worried that the baby
might drown if it was not born soon, as the expected date of delivery had just gone by.

The wish to delay the birth can also spring from fears about
possible damage during the birth. Lesley, in the last month of her
pregnancy, after a visit to the delivery rooms at the hospital, had
the following dream: 'I was in a train with my husband and we real-

ised that we were at the very front, that is, in the most dangerous position; we overheard the drivers talk of sick and hurt people who were in the last carriage.' In another part of the dream 'there was a human being, adult but the size of a child, covered in blood and wrapped up in white bandages.'

The psychoanalyst Marie Langer suggests that psychological factors involved in precipitating or delaying the date of birth include fears about the baby and either the intolerable need to find out or, on the contrary, the fear of finding out if the baby is healthy, fears which in turn relate to anxieties about the inside of the body and its 'badness'. (14)

Childbirth is often experienced by women as a situation in which they are being put to the test, and particularly in which their femininity is being put to the test. Some women are apprehensive of how they will behave at the birth, how they will cope with the pain, what emotions will surface. Some women cannot really believe that they are going to produce a child; it is with surprise that many a first-time mother looks at the baby to whom she has just given birth. Most women fear at least at some point in pregnancy that the baby will not be normal. These fears in a woman are linked to ideas about her body and its normality, about her femaleness and her genitals, about her ability to be 'triumphantly creative'. (15) Marie Langer traces the woman's fears of giving birth to a 'monster' back to what a woman feels to be her own 'monstrous feelings' of jealousy, rivalry and envy of her own mother. (16) At this moment of becoming a mother herself, a woman has to deal with her feelings about becoming equal with or even surpassing her mother, with her feelings about being separate yet identified with her mother, with her feelings about this baby which can so easily represent her own baby-self owned or disowned. To give birth to a healthy child is a reassuring experience for a woman and absolves her old feelings of guilt. Similarly to give birth without too much suffering is felt like the permission to be a woman. A positive experience in childbirth, where a woman can 'go-along' with her body processes rather than fight against them, can help a woman trust and value her body, sometimes for the first time.

By looking at the satisfaction in giving birth to a baby purely as a result of social conditioning and pressures, and as the only satisfaction afforded to women, feminists have tended to discard the deeper psycho-biological aspect of a woman's wish to confirm the goodness of her body, the healthy functioning of her female organs and her wish to come closer to, in a concrete way, her femaleness.

During pregnancy, women are often particularly aware of a sort of 'body time'. Hermine Demoriane in the diary of her pregnancy writes:

For the first time in my life I'm in step with the world. It's rather peaceful to have staked out a piece of time for oneself. It has a beginning and an end and it belongs to you. It makes you feel at home. I suppose dates are essentially feminine, our need and our fate. (17)

For some women the induction of labour is experienced as a violation of this sense of body time. To be induced because she has gone 'overtime' more often than not makes a woman feel that her body is being treated like a machine which must 'produce the goods' at a

standard time. She no longer gives birth according to her own spontaneous body processes and rhythm but the birth is monitored and
conducted by the medical staff and their machinery; the woman is
now only a piece of machinery herself, strapped in, hooked up and
injected into, standing between the baby and the outside world,
obstructing its passage and made to eject it or have it scooped out
of her. For a woman this feels a_long distance from the idea of
slowly helping her baby into the world at its own pace and her own
pace. It is probably this sense of violation of her own body
processes that makes many a woman say 'according to the doctor I
was late but not according to my dates....'

It is not a question of idealising the body processes and the
body's ability to give birth naturally without help in all cases,
but of pointing out the deep sense of violation many women feel when
their body is taken over in the ways I described, and their consequent sense of failure or inadequacy as women.

An example of this comes from Barbara's experience of the induction of her first labour. Barbara, whose second pregnancy I
followed closely, was aware of the effect of her experience in
childbirth on her handling of the baby. With her first child she
was induced on the day the baby was due for no urgent obstetrical
reason and delivered three days later with a vacuum extraction. 'As
I was coming down, I said to the doctor: "well, I couldn't even
manage that on my own...."' Although she had planned to breast
feed, when the time came she didn't feel able to ask to breast feed;
she felt she had failed at giving birth, how could she possibly
manage to feed the baby from her own body? She became depressed and
did not want another baby for some years. The birth of her second
child, on the contrary, was straightforward. She had no problem
breast feeding this second baby. The first experience had slotted
in with her fears about her ability to produce and nurture a baby
and, by shattering her confidence, made it even more difficult for
her to nurture the baby, whereas her second experience came to increase her confidence in herself and her trust in her own body, en-
abling her to breast feed and feel generally more able to deal with
her baby. Even one year after the birth of her second child she
still polarises her feelings towards the two children, the one who
makes her feel so inadequate and the one who makes her feel such a
good mother. Although other factors (such as the children's person-
alities) may be involved too, her experiences in childbirth and
consequent early relationships with her infants were certainly important in promoting such a split.

And in my research with a group of first-time mothers I found
that the women who coped well with having a baby were those who were
able to feel themselves to be active and creative at this time. Of
foremost importance is the woman's feeling that her body is able to
be productive, that it is able to 'give' birth to her baby. When a
woman can only have a child by her body being provoked into it, by
substances being continually pumped into it and more substances injected to dull the pain which has been thus increased, finally requiring the baby to be pulled out by forceps because she is para-
lysed from the waist down, she feels she hasn't given birth to her
baby. She also feels her body is unable to produce a baby. And in
a sense she is right. Creativity has been removed from her hands

into the hands of the doctor. One woman experienced induction as a rape (18) - it is in fact the ultimate passive obstetrical experience. In effect the doctor 'gives birth'. The practice of delivering women on their backs is a recent innovation made in the nineteenth century by the 'man midwives' (19) which, by being counterproductive to the easy delivery of the baby, provokes as well as evokes the passive role of the woman who 'is delivered of' her baby.

It seems to me important, in order to minimize the negative effects of obstetrical interventions and to restrict these interventions to a minimum, that the psychological aspects of, say, a delayed birth, as well as a woman's possible experience of obstetrical interventions, be taken into account by professional workers and given the weight they deserve. Obstetrical practices and interventions fit in, only too readily, with those fears a woman harbours of not being allowed or not being able to 'give' birth (for instance as a punishment for destructive feelings towards her mother), and this can have consequences on her long-term feelings about herself as a mother and her relationship with the baby.

The relationship of mother and infant

The case for or against certain obstetrical interventions and for or against childbirth in hospital is obviously not clear-cut, and partly depends on whether the emphasis is placed on the physical or the psychological side of childbirth (though this is further complicated by the fact that each can have an effect on the other). Seen as a 'rite de passage', childbirth in hospital can be helpful in offering a transition time to the woman, free from responsibilities, and can offer a haven in which she feels protected from unwelcome emotions. The other side of the coin is the restriction involved in an institutionalised setting with its strict hierarchical structure, rules and regulations. This has particularly striking effects in the days after the birth, as some women can tell.

Barbara described her experience after the birth of her baby:
I couldn't hold him when he was first born because I was flat on my back and I think ... they put him in a nursery just down the corridor and took me back to the ward and then my husband came, it was about two in the morning and he went and had a look at him and about four o'clock they said they would just put him in the other nursery with the other babies because he was sleeping quite well and they picked him up and gave him to me to hold. I remember them saying 'for Heavens sake, don't tell Sister' because they're not allowed to take them out for twenty-four hours, and I sat there feeling quite thrilled, for a little while anyway, I had about ten minutes I suppose, and then I went back to sleep and they put him in the nursery and the next day I fed him in the cot thing which they just tip up and you stick the bottle in, they don't want them picked up, and then I went back to the ward and there ... you don't actually get a set lecture on it, nobody comes and says 'you pick your baby up and feed him, burp him, change him and put him back down', but anyone that sat ... well, I used to sit with Peter, I couldn't put him down ... if you sat

for very long, they'd say 'you're going to have a lot of trouble
when you get home', this sort of thing ... and if the baby keeps
crying then they say 'Oh, so and so's baby, why don't you put him
or her into the nursery' ... they don't suggest you pick him up
and walk up and down and cuddle him, which is the obvious thing
to do, especially in hospital when you've got all the time in the
world. They say 'you should be resting, there's nothing wrong
with the baby' and so on and so on; they don't actually say to
you, you mustn't pick the baby up....

Barbara aptly perceives the atmosphere in the postnatal ward
where a spontaneous relationship between the new mother and her baby
is practically impossible. It is made quite clear to her that her
baby should only be picked up at specific times (feeding and
changing). The very layout of the ward with its high beds and
relatively low cots makes it very awkward for a woman to pick her
baby up. Comfortable chairs are sparse and generally for the use
of visitors. When I had my first child I was in a room on my own.
Nevertheless, every time a nurse came in I was told that I held the
baby in my arms too much and above all that I should certainly not
have her in bed with me. On one such occasion the nurse actually
took the baby from my arms and literally threw her into the cot.

Another woman describes the hours after the birth:

I remember feeling very strange, to have experienced the most
remarkable of all things, the birth of my first child and then
to be left all alone. First they took the baby into the nursery.
Then I was wheeled into my room, where my husband was able to
stay and chat for a while. But he had to work the next day, so
he needed some sleep. I was tired but too excited to sleep. So
there I was, alone, remembering the experience full of wonder and
amazement that we had all shared. But for the next few hours we
were not sharing. The hospital had separated us. (20)

Birth is a traumatic separation for mother and child and it is
natural for a mother to want to hold her child immediately and to
regain some of the closeness which she feels has been lost, as well
as to get to know the baby. As Terese Benedek puts it: ' ... the
infant is the object of the mother's receptive needs, she feels
"whole" with him and "empty" without him.' (21) For the woman who
is aware of such feelings in herself it is a painful experience to
have her baby removed from her. This can only accentuate an idea
she may harbour of not being allowed to have a baby, or the primitive fear of having her baby stolen from her, fears which stem from
the rivalrous situation with her own mother which I mentioned
earlier.

The reason for removing babies from mothers we are told, is to
allow mothers to rest. But the reason why mothers cannot rest with
their babies is that they are made to follow the rigid timetables of
an institutionalised setting. They cannot sleep when the baby
sleeps and awake when the baby awakes. It is not allowed. My
daughter had a habit of sleeping little during the night and her
best sleeping time was during the morning. In the morning, however,
when she and I wanted to sleep I was told that I had to take her to
the nursery for washing and dressing. Then I was told I had to wake
her up at specific times because this is when she ought to be hungry
regardless of her own internal rhythm. This indeed was tiring and
infuriating.

An example of the kind of mechanical approach which develops in an institutionalised setting where responsibilities are distributed according to a strict power structure, is the incident with the nurse who came to see, on my third day in, if I had filled in my chart. I had not been told about this chart and the nurse in panic produced a sheet and proceeded to ask me when I had fed the baby on the days since the birth. When I told her I could not remember as I had been demand feeding, she filled in the chart with what should have been the 'correct' feeding times because, she said, the paediatrician was coming in and would want to see the chart. Having created this perfect chart, she walked out satisfied. The paediatrician never asked to see it. The hierarchical structure creates a situation where those with little power apply rigid rules to their patients through a fear that leaves them unable to think flexibly.

The woman who has just had a baby is faced with a double message: as a mother, certainly on returning home, she is expected to be competent, strong, able to deal with her baby whatever the circumstances and to be devoted wholeheartedly to this baby. Yet, in hospital her baby is removed from her and becomes the property of the hospital as if the mother was incompetent or superfluous. She is expected to cope, yet has been prevented from coping. Here are created two opposite images, one of competence, one of incompetence. This is not far off from the split which I showed to be operating in the non-coping women in my study: an ideal of the perfect mother which the woman cannot possibly match up to, and the accompanying guilt. It is an internal problem, but one which is here greatly reinforced or even sometimes provoked by the external situation in the hospital setting, where it is made extremely difficult for a woman to learn to value herself as a mother.

That the woman needs to rest is undeniable, but the rest she needs is from household chores and the preparation of meals, not from being with her baby who, at this stage, still feels almost a part of herself. Women describe listening at night for a baby crying in the nursery, anguished and wondering if it is their baby. Apart from the cruelty of the situation, this can hardly be called a rest. In the case of a normal birth, a woman's feeling is one of excitement not fatigue, and her wish is to discover and explore her baby, not to rest in 'solitary confinement'.

Differences in the paediatric assessment of babies and the mother's feelings about their babies (in favour of extensive contact), even a year after the birth, have been found between those who were subjected to a rigid hospital routine and those for whom the hospital routines allowed extensive contact between mother and baby. (22) Martin Richards suggests (23) that one important factor is the mother's self-confidence. The more responsibility the mother is allowed, the sooner she becomes assured about her ability to look after the baby. Richards also suggests that the hospital gives the mother an implicit model of how she should care for her baby.

After all the hospital is run by paediatric and obstetric experts so it is reasonable for her to conclude that the pattern of contact laid down there is what modern science has proved to be best. Most mothers could hardly be expected to analyse the situation and conclude, as some social scientists have done, that the hospital routine is a product of the institutional structure and

the convenience of doctors and nurses and has very little to do
with the interests of either mother or baby.
Some decades earlier Glover made a similar point:

No doubt general practitioners could plead with some justification that their medical curriculum did not include instruction
in baby-psychology. But this does not prevent them laying down
laws on infant welfare that have obviously been based on physiological concepts of habit-formation. Witness for example the
fantastic theory that one should not pick up a child when it
cries; or that it must not be fed when it is hungry, unless the
hunger falls at a given moment in a time-table drawn up by
adults; or, again, that it must not be taken out of its cot at
night however audible the evidence of its misery. To these
pseudo-scientific varieties of obscurantism the nurse (alas!)
adds a superstitious and moralistic belief in the virtues of
discipline. So when the unfortunate mother comes along full of
tremors and trepidations about her capacity to handle the in-
calculable little bundle of life to which she has just given
birth, she falls an easy prey to authoritarian systems. It is
no exaggeration to say that this combination of physiological
obsession and moral inculcation of habits which suit the convenience of adults is responsible for more psychic suffering to
children than the physical neglect or positive cruelties of
earlier ages. (24)

In such a situation it seems that many mothers, going along with
the passive and subservient position women are often used to taking,
readily give up their mothering role and sensitivity to the baby's
needs to the competent parental figures, the nursing staff, who have
such definite ideas about what is right and wrong and how the baby
should be treated. For the woman it is an escape from her own inse-
curity, doubts, uncertainties about the best way of dealing with her
new baby, also sometimes an escape from the strong bond with the
baby and the upsurge of primitive emotions this involves.

Although there are differences between hospitals, it is important
to remember that a hospital is a totally different sort of organisation from a home, and that it cannot ever be like home. One woman
describes her awareness of such a difference:

So much was different the second time, like my husband was there
and I was at home and I didn't have any drugs, and when you've
had one you do feel more relaxed. I can remember when my first
child was born, in hospital, he was put in a cot, one of those
goldfish bowl type things and he was at the end of the delivery
bed and I thought what if he cries, I won't know what to do, what
shall I do ... not knowing anything, the uncertainty which wasn't
there with the second child to the same extent. Having him at
home, being responsible for him ... there was always somebody
else who'd take over in hospital, the so-called professionals who
were there to do it, whereas with him the midwife left at three
and we were on our own, they came in everyday but not on the same
basis. It was much more natural to feed him when he cried than
to sort of go and get a bottle.

Isabel Menzies's study of the nursing service of a general hospital (25) gives some understanding of the way in which nursing
practices and organisation come to operate as a defence against

anxiety. In the case of a general hospital the anxiety has to do
with the close contact and care of ill people. She found that
things were organised in such a way that anxiety in the nursing
staff was avoided rather than confronted and worked through. She
writes: 'little attempt is made positively to help the individual
confront the anxiety evoking experiences and, by doing so, to develop her capacity to tolerate and deal more effectively with
anxiety.' But also 'the social defense system itself arouses a good
deal of secondary anxiety as well as failing to alleviate primary
anxiety.'

In a maternity unit, nurses have to deal more specifically with
feelings related to pregnancy and childbirth, to life and death, to
rivalry and envy of the mother and baby, to ideas of good and bad
mothering and to their own mothering. A study of maternity units
would no doubt highlight the way in which such feelings are contained and avoided by the structure and organisation of the unit. But
also what Menzies describes in relation to the nursing staff holds
true for the mothers themselves. By the care of the baby being
taken over in the way it is done in hospital, the mother is encouraged to deal with anxiety by evasion, rather than by being
helped to confront and work through the anxieties. Thus the nursing
practices can encourage the mothers to defend against anxiety about
conflicts whose non-resolution can lead to difficulties such as
postnatal depression.

It is this sort of situation which makes many women say that the
week in hospital was like a 'holiday' - indeed a holiday, not just
in the sense of meals being prepared but in the sense that all
worries and conflicts are temporarily suspended, that no 'working
through' of difficulties takes place. This may seem pleasant at the
time, but what about in the long run? When I questioned them about
their experience in hospital, many women who had their baby in the
maternity unit at the top of a high-rise building in Brighton
answered that 'the view was beautiful'. Did nothing go on 'inside'?
It seems that what happens 'inside' the woman's mind was temporarily
suspended in that week in hospital. Unfortunately on returning
home, many mothers are overwhelmed by anxiety, the anxiety which has
been suppressed until then, with the detrimental effects this can
imply for mother and baby.

But in hospital too, the avoidance of anxiety is only partial,
and a secondary anxiety is provoked by the practices I have described. For example, the practice of removing the babies from the
mothers and taking over their care stimulates and enhances deep
fears about the baby being stolen by an envious woman at a time when
a woman needs to be helped to feel that she is not hated and envied
by other women for having a baby, and stimulates fears of not being
a good enough mother at a time when a woman needs to be helped to
feel that she can provide for her child. Such fears are primary
fears too and the perception of nurses (as envious, unhelpful or,
on the contrary, wonderful) will be greatly coloured by the pro-
jection of the woman's own feelings and unacceptable parts of herself. But the fears and feelings connected with the structure and
organisation of the unit can be seen as secondary anxiety. In other
words a certain amount of anxiety is avoided by the organisation of
the unit (and this accounts for some woman's remark that the week in

hospital was 'bliss') but, like any avoidance of anxiety in this sort of way, this is detrimental in the long run. Even at the time, it in no way eliminates all the anxiety. This anxiety often flares up in contagious waves in the postnatal ward at times of crisis and around rumours concerning the mismanagement of babies.

In my research on first pregnancies I found that the women who could express anxieties during pregnancy were better able to cope later on. Similarly I suggest that it is essential for women to be in touch with and learn to deal with the anxiety aroused by the early contact with the new baby in that first period in hospital. And this above all involves the babies not being taken over, the mother and baby relationship not being regimented.

Removing the babies at night and imposing a pre-set routine is also a way the nursing staff have of coping with another sort of anxiety, the anxiety aroused by spontaneity, desires, unruliness, individuality. And for the parents too, babies who comply to a strict regime and are 'good' and 'well trained' are often easier to cope with. But are they healthier children? And what about the feelings of inadequacy aroused in the mother when her baby does not comply with the set routine?

Taking over the care of the babies also stimulates a woman's feelings of passivity in the postnatal situation. I mentioned earlier my finding that the coping mother is also the one who feels herself to be active and creative and it is clear how the strict hospital practices work against the possibility of such feelings developing. The 'blues' so frequent in hospital and ascribed to hormonal changes are in my mind partly related to being prevented from this active elan towards the baby for which she has prepared herself with trepidation and tremulation for nine months, and the sense of futility and inadequacy which results from it. The mother loses trust in her spontaneity, she looks to the 'experts' for advice and learns to deal with her baby in a rule-bound aseptic fashion. One study of women suffering from a postnatal disturbance found that the majority of these women had an 'ambivalent identification with a controlling-rejecting mother' (26) and it is evident how for these women the nurses in such a setting would represent only too easily this controlling-rejecting mother.

Such a beginning is in danger of jeopardising the longer-term well being of the mother and her relationship with the baby. The woman comes home from hospital full of doubts, reliant on expert advice and often finds herself overwhelmed and unable to cope with this human being who doesn't fit into a set pattern. She listens to the baby breathing, terrified that he or she will die through her own incompetence.

It is in the area of breast feeding that the double messages a woman receives are best exemplified. A woman is told that she should breast feed her baby, that a breast-fed baby gets the best start in life and that a good mother does what is best for her baby and therefore breast feeds her baby. The woman who chooses to breast feed is then faced with a situation in which it is extremely difficult for her actually to succeed in breast feeding. I suggest this is the result of unconscious envy felt towards the mother and baby couple and their physical closeness in the feeding situation and of unconscious envy towards each of the partners, the mother who

feeds and the baby who is fed. The mother is told in hospital to
feed her baby every four hours and it is a rare mother whose breasts
receive sufficient stimulation in the beginning to produce enough
milk for the baby on a four-hourly schedule. In addition, breast
milk has a lower protein content than artificial milk and breast-fed
babies will tend to cry and demand a feed sooner than bottle-fed
babies. However, the mother is told that her breasts are not producing sufficient milk, that evidence for this is the fact that her
baby is demanding more frequent feeds and crying before the four
hours are up, and that she had better replace or supplement her milk
with bottle feeding 'for the good of the baby'. Many women are
heart-broken at having to make the change (unless they had chosen to
breast feed only because they felt they ought to), but the pressure
is too great for them to resist. Fitting in with their doubts about
themselves and their ability to satisfy their baby and doubts about
the goodness of what they produce, a new fear of starving their baby
forces them to make the change. For some women it is a great relief
to hand over the job of satisfying the baby to a bottle, where they
can measure exactly what the baby has taken and where they do not
feel responsible for the quality of the food. Though here too a
secondary anxiety sets in when the baby does not conform to the norm
and take the prescribed amount. It is thus that some women who
would have liked to breast feed miss out on what could have been a
most cherished experience.

In some hospitals the babies are even weighed before and after
most, if not all, feeds and the frequent finding of a rather small
gain in the baby's weight is given as evidence that the milk is
insufficient. Apart from the fact that this discounts the fact that
different babies take in different amounts, or the same baby takes
different amounts at different feeds, or that a baby might take
small but frequent feeds if allowed to do so, it is very trying for
the mother to be put to the test in this way. It is well-known that
how a woman is feeling has an influence on how much milk she produces (27) and for a woman who feels insecure about what she is able
to give, or about being successful in general, being put to the test
in such a way can be most inhibiting.

Many mothers feel insecure about their ability to produce good
milk and to satisfy their baby in this basic bodily way, and any
suggestion that their milk is insufficient is enough to discourage
them from persevering with trying to establish a satisfactory
breast-feeding pattern and relationship (which can and almost always
does take at least some weeks). Also in the hospital situation the
mother is intimidated from feeding her baby on demand and she is
often led to continue the rigid schedule once she returns home. If
she feeds her baby more frequently she feels she is doing something
wrong and tends to 'lie' about the number of feeds per day to the
Health Visitor. It takes a determined woman not to give up when
told that her baby is not getting enough milk because he or she
demands frequent feeds, and to feel that her milk is satisfying
to her baby.

When my daughter was a few weeks old my Health Visitor told me
that because the baby was demanding very frequent feeds I didn't
have enough milk. She then squeezed one of my breasts, looked
disapprovingly as there was no response and said cheerfully, 'Don't

worry dear, it's not because you can't breast feed your first child
that you won't be able to breast feed your next one', and then de-
parted. My confidence was somewhat shaken and I wondered if I was
starving my poor child (though she was pink and plump). Almost
guiltily I carried on with my frequent feeds, never admitting to
more than three- or four-hourly feeds to the Health Visitors I encountered, and breast fed to my and my daughter's pleasure for nine
whole months. It had never occurred to this Health Visitor that my
breasts might not yield any milk when she squeezed them, or that
they had recently been emptied by my daughter, or that if my
daughter looked healthy she must be getting enough, or that it is
possible to increase the number of feeds in order to increase the
intake of milk if the mother is happy with such a regime.

A large number of women believe that they have been unable to
breast feed their babies because their milk was insufficient or
inadequate, and many of these women experience it as a failure on
their part, or as an experience they and the baby missed out on.
This sense of failure slots into a sense of inadequacy as a mother
or to a sense of being like what they feel to be their own inadequate mothers. I suggest that the environmental pressures contribute largely to this by emphasising the value of breast feeding
while secretly undermining its success.

In all these different ways a woman is impeded from being a good,
spontaneous mother. Her baby is removed, she is made to adhere to
rigid timetables and warned not to spoil her baby. She is dis-
couraged from feeling confident about her ability to breast feed and
told to follow a regime which is likely to make breast feeding
unsuccessful. All the while the virtues of the good mother are held
up as a contrast to her own behaviour and the woman is likely to
feel a failure and guilty at her inadequacy. The split between the
perfect mother and the 'witch' which we saw operating in the non-
coping mother is thereby increased or even provoked. The woman then
wishes someone to take over and is relieved when the responsibility
is taken out of her hands; going home is dreaded and she delays the
moment when she will be left to cope alone.

Obviously different women will react differently to the same
situation and a woman for whom closeness with her baby is not wished
for, for instance, may welcome a system where contact between mother
and baby is closely regimented and regulated. Similarly, for the
woman whose sense of herself is easily devalued, any situation will
be compared with an ideal she has created and accentuate her
feelings of inadequacy. It is clear too that the external setting
will be perceived differently by women depending on the way they
feel about parental figures, and about being helped, the way they
deal with feelings such as rivalry and dependency, etc. Some women
may be able to cope in spite of the circumstances and others may get
severely depressed in spite of the best circumstances. But I am
suggesting that it is important to consider the reality of the external situation, in which it is made extremely difficult for any
woman to feel confirmed in a self-confident ability to mother,
because of the sabotage of hospital practices. The external circumstances can slot in with, articulate or increase the internal
problem which a woman faces in her need to resolve the good-bad
mother split and come to value herself as a mother if she is to cope

and 'grow' with the experience. Present medical practices surrounding childbirth and the postnatal period make it extremely difficult
for women to make the birth of a child into a positive experience,
(28) one that is confirming of their self-esteem, contributes to a
resolution of earlier splits and inaugurates a creative relationship
with their baby.

NOTES

1 A phrase coined by D.W.Winnicott to get away from the notion of
the perfect mother and to think in realistic terms.
2 'Expectant Fathers Leaflet', Margaret Williams, National
Childbirth Trust, 9 Queensborough Terrace, London W2.
3 'The Baby Book', ed. N.F.Morris, Charing Cross Obstetric De-
partment, Newbourne Publications Ltd.
4 For example Hook, D. and Marks, P.L. (1962), MMPI Characteristics of Pregnancy, 'J. Clin. Psychol.', 18, pp.316-17.
5 Lewis, Abigail (1951), 'An Interesting Condition: the Diary of
a Pregnant Woman', London, Odhams.
6 Demoriane, Hermine (1969), 'Life Star, A Diary of Nine Months',
London, Alan Ross.
7 Breen, D. (1975), 'The Birth of a First Child: Towards an
Understanding of Femininity', London, Tavistock Publications.
8 Beach, S.R., Henley, K., Peterson, A., Farr, M. (1955),
Husbands of Women with Postpartum Psychosis, 'J. Psych. Social
Work', April 1955, pp.165-9.
9 Main, T.F. (1958), 'A Fragment on Mothering', Davidson Clinic
Bulletin No.50.
10 Lomas, P. (1966), Ritualistic Elements in the Management of
Childbirth, 'Br. J. Med. Psychol.', 39, pp.207-13.
11 Gordon Bourne writes:
> Different advice is frequently given about care of the
> breasts in pregnancy and this advice changes not only from
> year to year, but also from town to town and country to
> country. It is often incorrectly stated that the nipples
> should be bathed in alcohol in order to 'harden the skin' or
> scrubbed with a soft brush. Nipples of normal shape and size
> require no care other than the daily use of soap and water.
> ('Pregnancy', London, Cassell 1972)

Niles Newton in 'Maternal Emotions' (Jackson, Mississippi,
Phronia Craft, 1955) writes:
> The standard advice to mothers is to keep their nipples
> clean. Nipples in our society are well protected by clothing
> from outside soil so that the 'dirt' mothers wash off is
> mostly the natural accumulation of sweat, sebum and milk.
> These nipple secretions are probably very important to the
> health of the nipple skin by preparing it to withstand vigor-
> ous sucking. Sweat with sebum has antibacterial properties.
> Sebum is an important contributor to the protective covering
> of the skin, and helps to keep the skin pliable.... The
> result of keeping the nipples 'clean' is damaged nipples and
> excruciating pain in some instances. An experimental study
> (Newton, N., 'J. Pediat.', 41, 1952) found that mothers

washing their nipples with soap solution had more nipple pain on all five days of their hospital stay than the control group who used only water. The pain was both more frequent and more extreme. Nipple pain in turn causes a limitation of sucking and the failure of breast feeding.

12   This is an opinion I encountered myself in hospital.

13   Richards, M.P.M. (1975), Innovation in Medical Practice: Obstetricians and the Induction of Labour in Britain, 'Soc. Sci. and Med.', vol.9, pp.595-602.

14   Langer, M., reviewed by Racamier, P.C. (1953), A propos de Maternité et sexe de Marie Langer, 'Evolution Psychiatrique', 3, pp.559-65.

15   Lomas, P. (1966), Ritualistic Elements in the Management of Childbirth, 'Br. J. Med. Psychol.', 39, pp.207-13.

16   Langer, M., reviewed by Racamier, P.C. (1953), A propos de Maternite et sexe de Marie Langer, 'Evolution Psychiatrique', 3, pp.559-65.

17   Demoriane, Hermine (1969), 'Life Star, A Diary of Nine Months', London, Alan Ross.

18   Kitzinger, S. (1975), Childbirth by Appointment, 'New Behaviour' (New Science Publications), vol.1, no.7, pp.254-97.

19   Richards, M.P.M. (1975), Innovation in Medical Practice: Obstetricians and the Induction of Labour in Britain, 'Soc. Sci. and Med.', vol.9, pp.595-602.

20   Quoted in 'Our Bodies, Our Selves', the Boston Women's Health Collective, New York, Simon and Schuster 1971, p.204.

21   Benedek, T. (1956), Toward the Biology of the Depressive Constellation, 'J. Amer. Psychoanal. Ass.', 4, pp.389-427.

22   Kennell, J.H. et al. (1974), Maternal Behaviour One Year After Early and Extended Post-Partum Contact, 'Develop. Med. Child. Neurol.', 16, 172-9, and Richards, M. (1975), Early Separation, in 'Child Alive', ed. Roger Lewin, London, Temple Smith.

23   Richards, M. (1975), Early Separation, in 'Child Alive', ed. Roger Lewin, London, Temple Smith.

24   Glover, E. (1941), Preface to 'The Nursing Couple', Middlemore, M., London, Hamish Hamilton.

25   Menzies, L. (1960), A Case-Study in the Functioning of Social Systems as a Defence against Anxiety, 'Human Relations', 13, no.2, pp.96-121.

26   Melges, F.T. (1968), Postpartum Psychiatric Syndromes, 'Psychosom. Med.', 30, 1, pp.95-108.

27   See for example J.K.Harfouche, The Importance of Breast Feeding, 'Journal of Tropical Pediatrics', September 1970, pp.135-75; or Niles Newton, Women's Feelings about Breast Feeding, in 'Maternal Emotions', Jackson, Mississippi, Phronia Craft, 1955, pp.43-59.

28   In my sample of 51 women, I rated 21 per cent of women (i.e. 11 women) as making a positive adjustment to the birth of their first child (Breen, D. (1975), 'The Birth of a First Child: Towards an Understanding of Femininity', London, Tavistock Publications).

THE WITCH

Female illnesses are often explained away as the inevitable concomi-
tants of phases of women's biological and social life cycles. The
activities of this Bori possession cult in dealing with the problem
of sterility or childlessness in Hausa society are discussed to
illustrate the importance and force of psychic structures in de-
termining a woman's notion of her self as healthy or sick.

Chapter 2

The Witch and her Devils

An exploration of the relationship
between femininity and illness

Susan Lipshitz

ACKNOWLEDGMENTS

Of the people who have helped me in the course of this book's production I want particularly to thank Dr Anne Whitehead for reading
this essay and for her suggestions of changes, and to express my
thanks to John McGreal, Mick Gold, John Mepham and Sybil Shine, for
their support and constructive criticism.

We cannot agree with those who see in psychopathological label-
ling but a mere variant of the 'psychological manoevres of
bourgeois ideologists' to hide fundamental economic facts.
Social psychology in itself did by no means ignore these facts
and was on the contrary born out of the impotence of exclusive
biological or economic materialism to explain fully the social
process in past and present. (1)

FEMININITY AND ILLNESS

Women are witchlike in being able to give birth to live beings and
are therefore possessors of an invisible internal substance that
provokes fear because it links them to another world than that of
male culture, thus requiring their limitation, containment or
punishment. Contrary to what is often assumed, this process of
placing women is not a natural consequence of biological sex differences. Formally, however, its basis may be equated with the capacity to procreate. In this essay my reference is to the psychological
construction of female sexuality in its 'feminine' form at the level
of the unconscious, and seen as part of familial ideology within
patriarchal culture. The psychic constraint of female sexuality
structures a split between sex for pleasure and sex for reproduction. The association between this splitting and illness amongst
women is explored in an attempt to show that by locating women in
patriarchal culture defined at the psychic level, their 'deviance'
in the form of witchcraft in seventeenth-century England and their

possession in Africa becomes comprehensible. My interpretation of
illness as symbolic draws on Freudian theory, and is also informed
by its elaboration by Lacan (2) and Kristeva (3) to further refer to
the processes of language.

Anthropologists seem to recognise that women are often seen as the
disruptive elements of the social order that usually gives the men
social and political power. In these ways cultures are always
patriarchal despite variations in patterns of residence, inheritance
laws or the independence and economic power of women in different
cultures and in different historical periods. When women are said
to be categorised as deviant in the sense of being not natural, ill
or peripheral, there is a tendency for the symbolic realm in which
they are located to be described simply as a reflection of biological and social structures, i.e. a reflection of the division of
labour based on the different biological functions of the sexes in
reproduction, and of an equivalent social division based on the fact
that it is men who exchange women. (4) The silence of women in
ethnographic data is said (5) to be due partly to women not having
language, as well as their being only rarely the informants of
(male) anthropologists. It is assumed that if (particularly female)
anthropologists talked with the tribal women, the latter would immediately reveal an autonomous female culture and its hitherto
hidden meaning. In a similar argument, (6) female possession,
located as a 'peripheral' religious activity, is assumed to make
use of women's oblique natural way of speaking through their fits
and trances. The terms of Ardener's 'problem of women' are altered
if we start by assuming not that there is a separate male culture
and a female one, either co-existing or locked in antagonistic
battle, that is mediated by institutions like illness or witchcraft
or possession. The cultural categories are here referred to the
psychic level, (7,8) in an effort to clarify the construction of the
meaning of sex difference in a patriarchal order that is taken to be
a symbolic order and one that constructs sexuality and masculinity
and femininity in particular ways. Patriarchal culture is here seen
as a system of symbolic meanings acquired by the individual subject
at the level of the conscious and the unconscious. Since both sexes
acquire this culture they will share categories, but their position
in relation to those categories will differ depending on their sex.
The self is always a sexed self that has a place even before its
birth in a family and in ideology. So a girl child has a place and
pregiven 'femininity' to refer to, neither of which can be freely
chosen by the individual. One way of understanding this is to
recognise that when the individual subject does not locate herself
(or himself) in the culture, they fall ill. It is one of the tasks
of this essay to show that this is not accidental but depends partly
on unarticulated standards of health and adulthood that measure
women against a 'masculinity' as an ideal in comparison with which
they are always found lacking.
    The construction of categories of self and other, the basic cate-
gories of difference, are structured as a question of sexual difference at the Oedipal moment. Lacan (9) claims there is always and
already a sexual difference, but the crucial force of language which

he equates with the Freudian unconscious makes the structuring of the ego an order imposed by linguistic processes. (10) This account enables us to analyse the patriarchal culture as an order that depends on the signifier of the phallus (not the physical genital organ nor a fantasy of it) for meaning. (11) The place of each subject in relation to that order depends on their relation of having or not-having the phallus. For a masculine and feminine subject, this in turn depends on their position in relation to the Freudian castration complex (see the Introduction of this book for expansion). Their resolution of their bisexuality and the structuring of their desire conditioned by the formation of the superego occur with the resolution of the complex at the Oedipal moment. Women's entry into the cultural order and into language then differs from that of men in some ways. It is defined as relatively less certain, less central and a more fragile transition from the realms of the Imaginary (12) and narcissism (13) into the Symbolic order. But in recognising that psychically women make an entry into culture, we are making nonsense of talk of an autonomous female realm or a feminine that is purely natural.

Since the language under discussion includes symbolism and does not reject it, and since all subjectivity is constructed meaning, there can be no meaningless natural realm to refer women to. I am concerned here with a particular disjunction in the cultural meaning of femininity; the contradictory demand for femininity and healthy adult functioning. The expression of this contradiction in the form of hysteria (14) and possession (dancing in the power of demons) or witchcraft (in the power of devils or evil spirits) makes the body the location of meaning. We witness a lack in language that is usually read as female constitutional weakness and not as accusation.

If we recognise that these forms of illness, possession and witchcraft are not simply attempts to seize power in the face of powerlessness, not simply illicit orgasms or rationalisations of desire, but are women's attempts to speak of the psychological limitation of their sexuality in its subordination to genitality and reproduction, we see them as ideological. For such activity, which makes little sense if it is seen as reflecting the strain of male-female social relations or as physical disease, can be understood as women's imaginary representation of their psychic condition to themselves. They are indicating the particular inflections of the construction of femininity. So to reclaim women witches or hysterics as examples of lost female power or lost healers, and to search for proof of their existence, as has some feminist literature, (15) is to take them too literally. In what follows, this essay examines the psychic conditions under which witches, etc. are fabricated so as to theorise the representation of procreative capacity and female sexuality on which female oppression is predicated.

THE WITCH AND WITCHCRAFT

Sing on and praise your true love, while I yawn,
For I've encountered her of whom you prate:

> I wish that dove a devil for a mate,
> Who'll leave her at the cross-road nicely tousled,
> Or an old goat from a Witches' Sabbath sousled,
> Who, when she murmurs her 'Good night my sweet',
> Will gallop off and answer with a bleat:
> You'll find a lad of flesh and blood too fine.
> For such a jilt, and then the laugh is mine.
> From me she gets no tribute or refrains,
> Except the sort to break her window panes. (16)

The witch in the examples discussed by historians and anthropologists is not imaginary. For as Thomas (17) points out in discussing English village witch belief of the sixteenth and seventeenth centuries, there were people who believed they could harm others merely by wishing to do so. It was Evans-Pritchard (18) who made a theoretical distinction at least between the psychic power to bewitch and the practice of sorcery that was based on the use of herbs and poisons. Amongst the Azande whom he studied, witchcraft was 'a psychic emanation from witchcraft substance which is believed to cause injury to health and property', and this substance was believed to be located near the liver. The witch need not be aware of the ability to do harm, it would just be activated by resentment. For men this was most likely to arise over political disputes and for women in disputes between co-wives in a family. Both these examples illustrate a general characteristic of witch beliefs, their use as explanation of misfortunes.

There was also, in Europe for example, a real fear that women witches could interfere with crops and disrupt an otherwise harmonious natural order of man and nature. According to Frazer, (19) widespread rituals such as fire-lighting and cleansing at midsummer were attempts to ward off witches.

> When we remember the great hold which the dread of witchcraft had
> on the popular European mind in all ages, we may suspect that the
> primary intention of all these fire festivals was simply to
> destroy or at all events to get rid of the witches, who were
> regarded as the causes of nearly all the misfortunes and calami-
> ties that befall men, their cattle and their crops.

The misfortune is thought to be inflicted by a person, considered socially deviant, a witch, who is both the enemy of the community's order and health, but is yet a part of the community. She (for witches are often women) is then a dangerous, demanding and yet close enemy. (20) The only people who have no such witch belief, the Mbuti pygmies, (21) seem also to have an informal social system, where there is no necessity that they stay within their band. They can then deal with evil or disruptive elements in the group by leaving or expelling someone physically and do not have to find means to contain that element, as is the case in more structured societies. (22) This implies that witchcraft belief can be comprehended within social relations rather than by reference to a metaphysical realm. Certainly accusations are usually localised and specific, as Thomas (23) lucidly shows in his analysis of the English cases. He suggests that those accused as witches in the villages of Essex were old women, often with no means of support and for whom a refusal of alms or the failure of social obligation often had desperate consequences. So the diviner of witchcraft helped the victim to find its source in a particular person who was often felt to be justifiably vindictive because of some previous injury suffered and was known to the victim. (Sometimes the witch was jilted by a lover, or said to have refused the advances of a man.) (24) The idea that times of transition, say, from an ideology of communal responsibility for the weak or outcast of society to one that favoured creating institutions for their care, would lead to an increase in witch accusations has not always been supported. Changing social and economic circumstances in parts of Africa that were rapidly becoming urbanised and industrialised did not always (25) lead to an increased attempt to state the old values and keep order through witchcraft.

Another way of understanding witchcraft in terms of social relations is to suggest that the often observed fact that women are witches or are the possessed is related to their limitation by rigidly defined social sex roles. Lewis, (26) for example, suggests that women all over the world use trance to demand goods and consideration that they are not usually granted. He suggests that this is a covert exercise of power aimed at rebalancing unequal power relations. However, it is striking that his examples do not include male groups of low status but are all female cases. Further, it is notable that while women are usually the accused, they are rarely the diviners of witchcraft. The only women who were diviners were those too old to bear children, or, because they were widowed, were conventionally not expected to have children, i.e. they were only diviners when they were not-feminine and the control of their procreative capacity was not socially demanded.

It is only if the misfortune being explained by witchcraft was unitary that one would expect one explanation to suffice. For example, if it was always the way communities dealt with 'mad' elements of their group, witchcraft and possession could be the location of pathology. There have been attempts to apply psychiatric categories to the behaviour of the witch (for example comparing her to a hysteric) or to the group who tolerates her, in an effort to assign health and right to one side. (27,28) The fruitlessness of this approach seems to have led some anthropologists to try to understand the activity within its own context, as other people's form of science and explanation of what was incredible or inexplicable for them. Often this would presuppose societal development as a series of stages where witchcraft was an early and primitive form of thought, as if it was an underdeveloped system of our scientific explanation. Of interest for this essay is the fact that so many women were witches and that their influence was thought of as psychic in both the historical and the cross-cultural examples mentioned. This evil activity was seen as irreconcilable with the 'sweet love' of romantic imagery, the woman who is chaste and good. The notion of femininity does not tolerate such aspects, which at different times will be represented as witchlike. There is no space to discuss further how this varies because the central concern of this essay is to discuss the shifts in psychic elements constructed by a woman's changing sense of self through her differing positions with age in the reproductive life cycle, and to relate these processes to the construction of the feminine in culture. For if women's sexuality is psychically organised for reproduction, it is their bisexuality (that might at times be equated with the pleasure they are denied) which is constrained and may be being expressed in defiance of the heterosexual imperative through some forms of witchcraft, possession and illness. Thus according to Freud (29) the spirit said to be afflicting them is a split-off part of their own mind and not a mysterious alien force. The splitting is accomplished by the repression of certain ideas about the self and sexuality that are returning. The fear being expressed by the women is that they are not being who they should be. It is the women's psychical relations to themselves that are being disrupted, relations that are not simply analysable as the other side of their social definition. In the discussion of possession amongst Hausa women that follows, the Bori cult's containment of sterile and childless women is interpreted to exemplify these ideas.

FEMALE POSSESSION IN THE BORI CULT

There are various forms of this cult in other parts of Africa in which women usually go into trance. (30) In the particular Nigerian example discussed here, men were forbidden to become initiates of the cult and could only belong as musicians. As they were often blind, these men, while central to the cult's activities, were also socially marginal. Cult initiates attribute their possession to attacks from intrusive forces from outside, other-worldly spirits recognised as part of the Hausa ideology. The origins of the cult, as recounted in mythology, are located in a postulated matriarchal era in which female goddesses were worshipped and sacred prostitution practised. In existing recorded histories Bori seems rather to have been influenced by clan practices - for example, it is known that Hausa women used to go into trance to prove their legitimate membership of a group. Several writers (Nicolas, (31) Onwuejeogwu, (32) Tremearne, (33)) relate how Bori became displaced in relation to the main ancestral religion, Anne, with the arrival of Islam in 1804. Today Islam remains the religion of the aristocracy, Anne refers to Hausa male activities of hunting, fishing and agriculture, and Bori deals with specifically female concerns with illness, sterility and fertility.

Under the rule of the Fulani, Hausa women were also socially displaced, for Muslim women are secluded after marriage and have little contact with people outside their own households. The household, 'gida', where a man and his several wives and children live is part of a patri-lineal clan group. Since residence is patrilocal, the women are always strangers living in an isolation that is further increased by their being 'in shame' in relation to their children who are sent to live with their maternal grandmothers after weaning. Adult women are only permitted the expression of tender feelings to their brother's children until their own reproduce. This is in contrast to their own relatively free childhood when they went to market, visited other villages and attended public ceremonies. At marriage this liberty is drastically curtailed: women at thirteen or fourteen years of age move from a situation where they are indulged by adults to one where they will spend their time working in the household, in rivalry with other wives for their husband's attention. It is these married women who are the candidates for the Bori, and only some of them get through the initiation. However they seem to form a large proportion of the female population, since Nicolas, (34) on whose study much of this account is based, interviewed sixty-two adepts of the cult, and they were part of a clan group of some several hundred people. She characterised the interviewees as a self-selected group of distressed and disturbing women who are outside of society before they join the Bori.

> Women come to the Bori cult because they are ill, because they are sterile, because their children are dying, in short because they have offended the gods who will not be appeased unless the women agree to become their 'mounts', the docile vehicles of their incarnation. (My translation.)

These misfortunes are not uncommon for the Hausa and everyone wears talismans to protect themselves from bad luck, illness, and death. The spirits invoked in the Bori ritual often represent types of illness (sleepiness, itching, limping, etc.) that are dramatically impersonated by the cult members. However it is only the women's solution, to cure ills by giving oneself to the gods, rather than by making a sacrifice or asking for pardon for the original offence assumed to have made the gods vindictively angry. To categorise this cult group as deviant is perhaps to accept the ideology of the culture about women's predisposition to sickness, not to recognise that sterility or illness are normal, and deviant only if fecundity is seen as normal. Further, the Hausa women saw Bori activities as a safeguard against what they call madness, and it is said that only those who refuse the call of the gods to join the Bori will go mad. Those who accept it and go through a seven-day-long initiation are said to be reborn and 'given a second chance'. This suggests the desperate position of women in a society where they only 'exist' as mothers. If they are sterile or childless through abortion or a child's death, they have no social value; the cult converts them from useless, harmful members of society to useful ones through its reaffirmation of their clan membership and through its providing them with healing skills. For (traditionally at least) it was a central aspect of a Bori woman's work to heal the sick, to protect people from the vagaries of the weather or disease, as well as to initiate other women.

Psychically, cultivating possession seems to mean the learning of absolute passivity in the presence of the gods. Here is an account of such possession written in 1850. (35)

> I found that one of our negresses, the wife of one of the servants, was performing Boree, the 'Devil', and working herself up into the belief that his Satanic Majesty had possession of her. She threw herself upon the ground in all directions, and imitated the cries of various animals. Her actions were, however, somewhat regulated by a man tapping upon a kettle with a piece of wood, beating time to her wild manoeuvres. After some delay, believing herself now possessed, and capable of performing her work, she went forward to half a dozen of our servants who were squatting on their hams ready to receive her. She then took each by the head and neck, and pressed their heads between her legs - they sitting, she standing - not in the most decent way, and made over them, with her whole body, certain inelegant

motions not to be mentioned. She then put their hands and arms behind their backs, and after several wild cries and jumps, and having for a moment thrown herself flat upon the ground, she declared to each and all their future - their fortune, good or bad.

She is a mare ridden by the gods and is honoured as the gods while she is thus possessed. The contact gives the woman emotional strength and expresses her anxiety about her sexuality through quite blatantly erotic dancing. What seems to be brought under control in Bori ideology and Bori rituals is a shift in the sterile woman's relation to herself, engendered psychologically when the element 'me-as-woman' is contradicted by the element 'me-as-sterile'. The sterility itself is not lethal, but its meaning is devastating for a woman since she values herself and represents the meaning of her social relations to herself in terms of her reproductive capacity. In Hausa culture the whole universe is thought to be composed of symbolic masculine and feminine principles and the sterile woman is not in her right place. Perhaps one of the ways the Bori helps such a woman is in its providing not only a group of like women with whom she can identify, but also in its recognition of their bisexuality. Part of the test of initiation is that a woman must watch, without a cry while other women dance together around her, violating the heterosexual cultural rule. In addition, the Bori ideology seems to recognise female activity and that women have sexual desire even outside of the legitimating structure of marriage. That is to say, I think one can interpret Bori women's 'liberty', both their economic independence and their resistance to being put into purdah, as well as their resorting to prostitution (36) when they are between marriages, as social activities that have psychic resonances. So while the Bori cult may well mediate relations between humans and gods, between women normally in competition in their households and between men and women, it also symbolically mediates unconscious conflicts, as Nicolas claims. For a sterile woman, the possibility of seeing herself as a healer rather than one of the sick in need of healing offers the possibility of her constructing herself as adult and normal in a situation where being feminine and a real woman are supposedly predicated on her fertility.

THE INTERPRETATION OF SYMPTOMS AND THE QUESTION OF FEMININITY

The understanding that symptomatic behaviours are constructed and symbolic meanings that can be deciphered, comes from psychoanalysis. Freud (37) showed in his early work with hysterical women patients that their symptoms were meaningful if approached with an expectation of their rationality, although it is not that of formal logic. He related this ordering to the structuring force of repressed ideas about sexuality, ideas that are kept out of consciousness often by the formation of symptoms. Freud justified postulating a place called the unconscious where these ideas are located because it enables us to explain what are otherwise inexplicable 'gaps' in the experience of both healthy and sick people.

In everyday life these eruptions include dreams (38) and parapraxes, (39) and in more extreme form they are manifest as delusions, paralyses, theatrical rituals and convulsions. We have to 'presuppose other acts of which, nevertheless, consciousness affords no evidence', (40) or else there can be no meaningful connection between conscious acts which are only partly accessible to us. Whether the latent aspect of consciousness is mind or body has been much debated; Freud himself is inconsistent, at times rejecting a psycho-physical parallelism and at other times not. Now if, for example, that 'other place' is thought to be composed of several mental unconsciouses, there can be only infinite regress in any explanation and no mental structure can be postulated. Part of Freud's answer to the problem of locating the unconscious was to demonstrate that the transformational processes of displacement and condensation operated in the production of dreams and of symptoms, and that both were overdetermined meanings. In the last instance Freud thought that ideas that referred to sexuality were the most important determinants of symptoms, although he did recognise the effects of organic processes.

This work contributes to the possibility of articulating the relationship between femininity and illness. (41,42) For one of the phenomenal forms of 'femininity' in twentieth-century European society at least, is what is called mental illness. Many more women than men are ill in this way and diagnosed as depressives or psychoneurotics; illnesses that are comprehensible as states of retreat or the turning in upon themselves of anger or frustration as might be expected from the stereotype of femininity. Since these illnesses are usually expressed as physical symptoms (tiredness, sleeplessness, crying, weight loss, etc.), they are assimilated to a medical model of disease, (43) with all the subsequent implications that the problem can be isolated, diagnosed, treated and cured. What is problematic becomes ephemeral, and contained within dominant notions of scientific medicine. A medical model of madness implies that the patient's body gets specialist medical and nursing care, and may be subjected to surgical procedures, rather than that the illness is a psychological one related to problems of living. I would argue, however, that the changes women experience in body shape, size and weight throughout their lives, and that are normal, only have meaning in terms of their context as pathological or normal.

In what we perceive as the normal transitions of identity in other cultures, like the Bemba, (44) Bakweri (45) or Gisu, (46) where the meaning of maturational changes at puberty, childbirth or marriage have been shown to be symbolically constructed for women through various rituals, this seems easier to see. It also seems clear that the rituals refer to the female reproductive cycle and to the containment of female sexual power and its dangers. The Bemba girl, through the dancing of her Chisungu, (47) becomes part of the adult female group of her society. Her submission to authority, her flexibility and her fertility are all emphasised, combining to prepare her for her wifely duties and her role in reproduction. The constraint of women's sexual expression seems overtly to be structured through the emphasis on legitimate pregnancy, the special mystical bond between man and wife and the sexual right of the husband. We learn further, from another culture's puberty ceremony in Malabar, (48) that biological and social identity changes do not have to coincide. It was essential only that the tali-tying be accomplished when the age of onset of menstruation had been reached, and that it preceded the physical event. Otherwise the woman would be said to be polluting, a witch and dangerous for a man to marry because her sexuality would be out of his control.

I suggest that at the psychic level these rituals are structuring sexual difference, reiterating the incest taboo and heterosexuality. The processes of normal and pathological transition were intentionally elided so far, so as to make explicit their similarity. For once the manifestations of illness, possession or witchcraft are no longer compared at the level of behaviour, the polarisation of what is 'illness' and what is 'health' becomes more difficult to maintain. The combination of elements constructing the meaning of adulthood, health and femininity, is what is of interest, a process that seems to be quite complex. The following account of Freud's work on hysteria with Breuer is an example of such a process. (49)

Hysteria tended to be manifest in girls at puberty, a conjunction whose regularity made Breuer (50) ask himself whether the 'process of pubertal development itself' did not create the illness. He recognised that girls approaching maturity had to cope with their sexual feelings as well as the social limitation of their activities. Hysteria was not then a moral weakness or degeneracy, 'innate psychical weakness', since, he noted, many gifted adolescents fell ill including 'girls who get out of bed at night so as secretly to carry on some study that their parents have forbidden from fear of their overworking'. He saw the conflicts that led to illness at this time as arising out of the girls' attempts to reconcile their feelings of sexual desire with their internal standards of purity. The only other possibilities open to them were to ignore the question of sexuality altogether or to accept it like a boy (that is, to be explored). None could lead to a conflict-free resolution. The girl 'senses in Eros the terrible power which governs and decides her destiny and she is frightened by it', Breuer says. (51) Similar conflicts were said to be aroused in women having their first sexual experience in marriage and the development of hysteria at these times is attributed to the problematic construction of female sexuality. For 'apart from sick-nursing, no psychical factor is so well calculated to produce reveries charged with affect, as are the longings of a person in love. And over and above this the sexual orgasm itself, with its wealth of affect and its restrictions of consciousness, is closely akin to hypnoid states'. (52) Such states are only more developed in hysterical attacks whose 'psychical content ... consists partly in ... the ideas which have been fended off in waking life and repressed from consciousness. Cf. the hysterical deliria in saints and nuns, continent women and well-brought up children.' (53)

In Anna O's case such fits took the form of anaesthesia of the limbs, convulsions, 'naughty' behaviour like throwing cushions, mood changes and her frightening hallucinations of black snakes 'which was how she saw her hair, ribbons and similar things'. When she was lucid Anna told herself at times not to be so silly, and then she complained that she was going blind and deaf, and of 'having two selves, a real one and an evil one which forced her to behave badly and so on'. (54) Breuer's analysis of Anna helped her to make conscious and to articulate conflicts between her anxiety for her

sick father and her wish to join a dance next door (thus wishing him
away or dead) and to be free to follow her desire for pleasure.
This was one of the bad thoughts she needed to repress that her
recalling helped to make less intolerable, leading to the loss of
her symptoms. In similar ways most of the cases of Freud or Breuer
(e.g. Freud's work with Elisabeth von R. who was suffering from
guilt at feeling sexual desire at the same time as she was nursing
her ill father) refer to Oedipal wishes or to conflicts about sexuality that are censored and lead to illness of this kind. These examples are quoted not to suggest that all illness originates in
traumatic memories that are then repressed and, once remembered,
lead to health. For in Freud's later work it became clear that the
deciphering of symptoms could be accomplished without any use of
hypnosis, the laying on of hands or any other physical means,
through the speaking of the problem within the transference relationship. (55,56)

The elements of the 'problem' became considered as fantasies that
had as powerful and material an effect as 'real' traumatic events
but were also autonomous from such events. Breuer elaborated, in a
way that it seems likely Freud agreed with, how the devils of their
hysterical women patients were mental events, not evil spirits.

> The split-off mind is the devil with which the unsophisticated
> observation of early superstitious times believed that these
> patients were possessed. It is true that a spirit alien to the
> patient's waking consciousness holds sway in him, but the spirit
> is not in fact an alien one, but a part of his own. (57)

This account of the devils leaves us no longer surprised by the
sexual overtones of the Bori seizure, of the grand hysterical
orgasmic arc of Charcot's patients, and their similarity to the
dancing of possessed nuns called witches or consorts of the Devil
in seventeenth-century European literature and the earlier demon-
ologies.

I want finally to illustrate the association of femininity,
illness and the constraint of female sexuality at the psychic level
with the example of the menopause and how it might be interpreted.
It should indicate that to see 'the normal as but a variant of the
concept of the good and the proper', (58) is inadequate unless the
way goodness and health are constructed to a masculine standard is
taken into account. Menopausal depression is fairly common in
England and America today and has been interpreted by feminist
writers (59) to refer to the loss of women's most socially valued
capacity, that of producing children. In some cultures this is ex-
changed for the gain of rights to civic status and political power
from which women were previously excluded. Or, as was mentioned
earlier, women can become shamans, witchdoctors or controllers of
spirit forces legitimately in some cultures. It is suggested here
that such compensatory social power will not alter the relations
between masculine and feminine elements determined at the earliest
structuring of the sexed self. That structuring can perhaps best be
described as 'recalled by' events in the subject's history that
resurrect the issue of sexual difference and a woman's placing in
relation to the culture. In so far as menopause and sterility might
be said to have the same psychic meaning in some ways, the shift in
relations between psychic elements they precipitate should be said

not to be due to age or hormonal changes. Thus menopause or sterility could be described as resurrecting guilt about sexuality and
its expression outside the legitimating structures of marriage and
the family (the split that was set up at puberty, for example). The
middle-aged or sterile woman might be experiencing her marriage as
incestuous, (60) for her husband becomes taboo, since he can no
longer be thought of as a potential father of her children, and like
her own infantile wishes for her forbidden father he is not legitimately desired. This may increase guilt, yet could also lead to
relief since the freeing of her sexual expression from the demand,
or possibility of reproduction might free the woman from a necessary
concern with contraception or the possibility of conception. It
seems that the image of the bad mother, displaced by the woman's own
maternity, may be revived with barrenness that faces her with the
process of ageing and inevitable death. And the loss of the self
represented by these changes may have to be mourned if there is to
be growth or health. It is perhaps a measure of the inflection of
our construction of femininity that this shift which could free the
woman's greater pleasure is bound up with and dominated by its
normal coincidence with her loss of social value, her illness and
despair.

So the location of the meaning of femininity in the unconscious
makes it part of the cultural construction of sex difference and
female sexuality, thus indicating why it is not simply dissoluble
by changes in social or economic circumstances, (61) nor can be
expected to vary with women's social power. This essay does propose
that such structures be taken into account by women's ideological
struggle and in the further development of theory.

NOTES

1 Ackerknecht, E.H., Psychopathology, Primitive Medicine and
   Culture, 'Bulletin of the History of Medicine', vol.14, no.1,
   1943.
2 Lacan, J., 'Ecrits', Editions du Seuil, 1966.
3 Kristeva, J., 'Des Chinoises', Editions des Femmes, 1974. She
   suggests the witch and the hysteric are located outside of the
   dominant language order, i.e. displaced from the unified symbolic system of signs. She sees the setting up of a division,
   categorically and socially, between the sexes, as necessitating
   the location of polymorphousness and excess in the other, in
   women. Women end up again in the realms of pleasure and nature,
   while men are cultural beings, a classification that seems to
   be at risk of reproducing an essentialist position on masculinity and femininity, despite its attempts not to.
4 Lévi-Strauss, C., 'Elementary Structures of Kinship', Allen
   Lane, 1968.
5 Ardener, E., Belief and the Problem of Women, in 'The Interpretation of Ritual', ed. La Fontaine, J.S., Tavistock, 1972. It
   is important to see the distinction between Ardener's use of the
   notion of language, as spoken words, and its use, as above, to
   refer to linguistic categories and the signifying practices they
   make possible.

6   Lewis, I.M., 'Ecstatic Religion', Penguin, 1971. Lewis suggests that witchcraft and possession are not so dissimilar, as in both cases women are subject to spirit attacks. The difference, he says, is that in the former, there is a direct attempt to disrupt extant social relations whereas in the latter the accusation is oblique, indirect, and a demand for attention rather than a challenge. Possession for him is a transcendental experience, the 'seizure of man by divinity', divinities that in the cases of female possession he discusses, are amoral and peripheral, as are their victims in society.

7   Althusser, L., 'Lenin and Philosophy', New Left Books, 1971. In his essay on 'Freud and Lacan' Althusser postulates a distinct object of analysis for the science of psychoanalysis, i.e. the unconscious. He accepts Lacan's reduction of the unconscious to language, and this enables him to connect ideology to subjectivity.

8   Laplanche, J. and Pontalis, J.-B., Fantasy and the Origins of Sexuality, 'International Journal of Psychoanalysis', vol.49, part 1, 1968. This paper really struggles with the problematic construction of a 'psychic' level, within psychoanalytic theory, one that evades the trap of placing the unconscious as mind or body, through an argument for the force of fantasy in mental life.

9   Lacan, J., 'Some Reflections on the Ego', Lecture to the British Psychoanalytic Society, May 1951.

10 Lacan, J., The Mirror Phase, 'New Left Review', 1968.

11 Lacan, J., The Signification of the Phallus, in 'Ecrits', op. cit.

12 The Imaginary is that order in which the image of the counterpart is dominant. It has been confused with primary narcissism, where the infant is said to take itself as love object in a state where self and other are not differentiated. Moving from the realms of the Imaginary to the Symbolic in Lacan means something like moving from considering resemblances between things to the use of language in a structured symbolic system where there can be no simple isomorphism between signifier and signified.

13 Freud, S., 'On Narcissism', in 'The Complete Psychological Works of Sigmund Freud', Standard Edition, Hogarth Press and the Institute of Psycho-analysis, 1974.

14 Hysteria - in conversion hysteria psychical conflict is said to be expressed symbolically in somatic symptoms. Psychically certain kinds of identification and mechanisms, like repression, and Oedipal conflicts, predominate. See Laplanche, J. and Pontalis, J.-B., 'The Language of Psychoanalysis', Hogarth Press, 1973.

15 Ehrenreich, B. and English, D., 'Witches, Midwives and Nurses', Glass Mountain Pamphlet, no.1, 1974.

16 Goethe, J.W., 'Faust', Penguin edn, 1975.

17 Thomas, K., Anthropology and the Study of English Witchcraft, in Douglas, M., 'Witchcraft Confessions and Accusations', Tavistock, 1970.

18 Evans-Pritchard, E.E., 'Witchcraft, Oracle and Magic among the Azande', Oxford University Press, 1937.

19 Frazer, J.G., 'The Golden Bough', Macmillan, 1971 edn.
20 Douglas, op.cit.
21 Turnbull, C., 'Wayward Servants', Natural History Press, New York, 1965.
22 My thanks to Anne Whitehead for this insight.
23 Thomas, K., op.cit.
24 Unsuccessful love affairs were often the catalyst for women becoming enthusiastic preachers. Besides Joanna Southcott, mentioned in the Free Woman, chapter 6 in this volume, this was true for Caterina Fagerberg and Elisabeth de Ranfaing in Sweden, for example.
25 Mayer, P., cited in Douglas, op.cit. p.137, does support this hypothesis.
26 Lewis, I.M., A Structural Approach to Witchcraft and Possession, in Douglas, op.cit.
27 Sargant, W., 'The Mind Possessed', Heinemann, 1973.
28 Bateson, G. and Mead, M., 'Balinese Character', 1942, cited in Lewis, I.K., Note 6, op.cit.
29 Freud, S. and Breuer, J., 'Studies in Hysteria', Basic Books, New York, 1959.
30 Other Bori groups have been located in Algeria, Tunisia, Niger and in similar form such groups exist in Dahomey and Sierra Leone, Senegal and Ethiopia.
31 Nicolas, J., Les Juments des dieux, in 'Etudes Nigeriennes', vol.21, 1967.
32 Onwuejeogwu, M., Cult of the Bori Spirits among the Hausa, in Douglas, M. and Kabery, P. eds, 'Man in Africa', Tavistock, 1969.
33 Tremearne, A.J.N., 'Hausa Superstitions and Customs', Bale and Danielsson, 1913.
34 Nicolas, op.cit.
35 Tremearne quotes an earlier writer, Richardson.
36 This form of prostitution was more like being a courtesan than a woman of the streets; the Hausa Bori women lived in groups and received men as friends not only as clients. Their freedom to thus converse with men as equals, to drink and smoke and to live alone, was part of the strength of support the Bori gave its members to stand out against conventional morality, according to Nicolas. Most of these women were between marriages, and tended to remarry within a few years.
37 Freud and Breuer, op.cit.
38 Freud, S., 'The Interpretation of Dreams', 'Complete Works', vols 4 and 5.
39 Freud, S., 'The Psychopathology of Everyday Life', 'Complete Works', vol.6.
40 Freud, S., 'The Unconscious', 'Complete Works', vol.14.
41 Lipshitz, S., Women and Psychiatry, in 'The Sex Role System', eds Hartnett, O. and Chetwynd, J., Routledge & Kegan Paul, 1977.
42 Chesler, P., 'Women and Madness', Doubleday, New York, 1971.
43 Siegler, M. and Osmond, H., Models of Madness, 'British Journal of Psychiatry', 112, 1966, pp.1193-203.
44 Richards, A.I., 'Chisungu', Faber & Faber, 1956.
45 Ardener, op.cit.
46 La Fontaine, J., Ritualisation of Women's Life Crises in Bugisu, in La Fontaine, op.cit.

47   Richards, op.cit.
48   Gough, K., Female Initiation Rites on the Malabar Coast,
     'Journal of the Royal Anthropological Institute', no.85, 1955.
     Tali-tying is the symbolic defloration of the young girl, and
     marks her change in status by a ritual marriage. The tali is
     a gold ornament strung on a thread of white silk, that is tied
     around the girl's neck. It is shaped like the leaf of a pipal
     tree, said to symbolise male creative power, and barren women
     are sent to march around it in order to become fertile. Gough
     relates the rite to the horror of incest, that leads a girl's
     natal kinsmen to renounce their rights in her mature sexuality
     before she is mature. They thus split off her sexuality from
     her capacity for domestic service and for procreation.
49   Freud and Breuer, op.cit.
50   Breuer, in Freud and Breuer, op.cit.
51   Ibid.
52   Ibid.
53   Freud and Breuer, op.cit.
54   Breuer, in Freud and Breuer, op.cit.
55   Freud, S., 'Dora', 'Complete Works', vol.7.
56   Freud, S., 'Observations on Transference Love', 'Complete
     Works', vol.12.
57   Breuer, in Freud and Breuer, op.cit.
58   Young, K., quoted in Ackerknecht, op.cit.
59   Bart, P., Depression in Middle-aged Women, in Bardwick, J.M.,
     ed., 'Readings on the Psychology of Women', Harper and Row,
     1972.
60   Heimann, P. and Isaacs, S., Regression, in 'Developments in
     Psychoanalysis', no.43, Hogarth Press, 1952.
61   Coward, R., Lipshitz, S. and Cowie, E., 'Psychoanalysis and
     Patriarchal Structures', Paper to the Feminist Theory Conference
     on the Patriarchy, London, 1976.

THE WHORE

The legendary fascination of prostitution and the image of the whore
are related here to the power of an unconscious image of a feared,
evil and sexual woman. Her place in the ideology of Peruvian
machismo culture and in a particular brothel, whose practices are
discussed in terms of their symbolic significance, is linked to the
infant's experience of good and bad aspects of the mother.

Chapter 3

The Whore in Peru

The splitting of women into good
and bad and the isolation of the
prostitute

Katherine Arnold

ACKNOWLEDGMENTS

With thanks to George Primov for permission to quote this material.

INTRODUCTION

Women are apparently divided and defined by their relationship to
men into the good and the bad: the prostitute being the classic
example of the bad woman. A woman becomes a prostitute when she
offers her body for hire to any man who will pay for her sexual
services. By doing this she is separated from the respectable
women, the wives, mothers and daughters of her clients. The way a
woman uses her sexuality is taken by most cultures to be one of the
most important things about her.
    Men are not categorised or restricted socially by their sexual
behaviour to the same extent as women. In Western society, homosexuality and paedophilia are perhaps the only sexual practices that
disqualify men from certain social positions.
    There are social reasons for and explanations of the control of
women's sexuality. Women's sexual behaviour is seen as more socially important partly because women give birth. In a society in which
women and children depend economically upon men for economic support
and the inheritance of position and status, men are concerned with
legitimacy and are able to require women to be sexual.
    But there are implied assumptions behind these systems of control
of women's sexuality which cannot be understood in social terms.
For instance, women are not seen as able or willing to control themselves. They are suspected of harbouring desires which are inimical
to the smooth functioning of patriarchal society. To understand the
force of these ideas it is necessary to turn to psychology and the
way individual fantasies relate to social practices. These two
levels, the social and the individual, are interwoven throughout
this paper.
    Prostitutes are required to satisfy a fantasy that someone will
fulfil any desire a man may have. This fantasy is created when the

infant feels his mother can satisfy his every need, and re-emerges
in the adult male in such forms as the belief in a 'golden-hearted
whore'. Like the mother, the whore can never satisfy her clients
totally, and she is then seen as a tantalising, frustrating and evil
person.

This dual view of women is not normally accessible to us since it
is unconscious and often disowned. The form in which prostitution
is institutionalised in a particular society can be analysed to
reveal these different views of women and their sexuality, and also
serves to guard against the twin dangers of dependency and loss
which are the greatest infantile fears remaining inside each of us.

I shall present the material I collected in a city of southern
Peru, during ten months of field work there between 1972 and 1974.
(1) Much of my information is from the women of the house, in particular the administrator, and I am indebted to them for their time
and help, without which this paper could not have been written.

PERUVIAN 'MESTIZO' SOCIETY'S EXPECTATIONS OF MEN AND WOMEN

Peru has a culture in which men strive to achieve 'machismo'. The
'macho' (a man who has got 'machismo') is strong and self-reliant.
He is able to protect and provide for his dependents, and other men
leave his womenfolk alone as they fear the 'macho' and his anger.
However, the 'macho' may well try to seduce their wives and
daughters, and thus demonstrate his social and moral superiority.
The sexual behaviour of the women of his family is of great importance to any man's prestige and social position. As the family
is a social unit which is judged as a whole, the woman must behave
according to certain rules if she wants herself and her relatives
to be well-regarded.

It seems as if the woman is totally dependent upon the man for
economic support and social protection - but when the situation is
considered more closely it is apparent that there is a mutual dependency. The woman has the power, if she wishes, to attack her
husband's sexual reputation by sleeping with another man, particularly one of lower status than her husband.

Like their sisters in other parts of the world, Peruvian women
are still expected, in the geographical and social area I studied,
to be weak and childlike. They are also watched and controlled by
men, who fear women's supposed desire for sexual promiscuity.
Interestingly, this sort of veil and pretence can only persist in
disguising the nature of women when men can economically afford to
restrict their women. Lower-class women have to work and often
support their families by trading in the market. (2) The middle
('mestizo') class is able to live more closely by the ideals of
'machismo', because middle-class women are not required to contribute economically to the family. Their contribution to the
social standing of the family is to be manipulated by men as symbols
of male prestige and status, which requires that women are kept in a
position of dependency and childishness.

In the city I lived in, middle-class women could expect to be
chaperoned. The women viewed this as a joke, a compliment, or a
great nuisance, depending upon their own temperaments, and those of

their spouses who determined how the chaperoning was done. Women
escape this supervision if their husbands die, at which crisis one
woman I knew well emerged as an extremely competent breadwinner and
organiser of her household. This 'señora' is an elderly widow who
is proud of her origins in one of the old, aristocratic families of
the city. It was from her that I heard many stories and gossip
which showed me how strongly the views that women are both weak
and yet are to be feared and despised for their ability to lead
men into sexual misbehaviour are held throughout the city.

SEXUALITY - 'GOOD' AND 'BAD' WOMEN

There were many inconsistencies in the beliefs about sexuality. I
was told about a maid who sat on a man's bed. She was said to be
leading him on, and she would get all she deserved. Later when a
different maid sat on the same man's bed, she was also accused of
leading him on, but this time the 'señora' said, 'What does a man
want more than a woman of any class?' Sexuality in general is seen
as being out of control. The important loss of prestige suffered by
a woman who is seduced, and the corresponding gain for the man involved, is hinted at here. A man can benefit from any seduction he
achieves, even if the woman is his servant and in his pay. The
seduction of a prostitute gives kudos to the client.

Men are also stereotyped and restricted by the 'machismo' ethos
of the society. They are expected to be sexually unfaithful to
their wives, and are suspect if they are not seen to be so. The
same 'señora' told me the story of a high-class woman whose husband
slept with the servant woman. She complained of his conduct to her
brother who came to defend his sister's position. He was given
turkey to eat every day until he became sick of the luxury and asked
his brother-in-law why they were obliged to dine on turkey all the
time. He was told that now he could see why a man needed other
women. Even if their wives were good wives and satisfactory in
every other way, variety is a necessity in sexuality.

For respectable women, however, sex is a part of marriage, which
is a serious business. An unmarried woman of the middle class of
this provincial city leads a very circumscribed life, and is an
object of pity and concern to her relatives. This was still the
case even though women could work as teachers, or in offices and
banks. The aim in life of most of the women of this class is to be
married and supported by their husbands. They would then have
children who were looked after by maids, who in the past often came
from the Indian villages of the family's estates. This was how the
early years of the present adult middle-class population were spent,
and although the situation is now changing, the old families of the
city jealously guard their position and try to maintain the old
traditions.

Sexual activity between husband and wife would seem to be restricted by tradition to the missionary position - both partners lie
horizontally and the man is above the woman. As one of the exotic,
more expensive forms of sexual activity in the brothel is sex in the
nude, it seems probable that in bourgeois marriages both partners
remove only the minimum amount of clothing.

The woman in the home is required to be sexless - like the
Madonna mother who plays such an important role in the religious
life of the city. The myth that women's sexuality can be avoided
by all concerned, and that some sort of sexless conception will
create children, receives ardent support. This myth is subscribed
to by men and women, and seems to hide a deep fear of women's sexual
powers that must be kept outside the home and family as they are
seen as potentially so dangerous. Octavio Paz describes a Latin
American view of women - 'Woman is a domesticated wild animal,
lecherous and sinful from birth, who must be subdued with stick and
guided by the "reins of religion"' (1961, p.36). The potential,
dangerous sexual powers of the unsubdued woman are focused in the
prostitute, who therefore becomes a person of great importance and
fascination.

Besides the Peruvian interest in the Madonna, Mary Magdalene was
also a figure who attracted attention. I was told by a woman of
the city that one of the prostitutes walked in the Easter procession, representing Mary Magdalene. This was not true, in fact,
but provides an illustration of a continual, open interest in
prostitution. Exaggerated stories were also circulated, both of
the prostitute's wealth and her exploitation by the owner of the
brothel. The belief was that the women were all foreigners,
although legislation in fact required them all to be Peruvian.
I was warned by a Peruvian woman anthropologist that I would be
in danger of being beaten up in the house. This sort of miscon-
ception illuminates the enormous split in the society's images of
women - on the one hand the safe, asexual wife at home, and on the
other the wild, exotic, dangerous and debased woman believed to
exist in the brothel. The respectable women seem to want to
polarise this split, and need the sexual woman to behave in even
more extreme ways than she actually does.

Another aspect of this split is revealed by the belief that men
are unable to work if they do not have access to the body of a bad,
sexual woman. The oil camps which exist in the jungle have to be
visited by a prostitute at regular intervals or work simply grinds
to a halt. The sexuality of women provides a sort of life force
which is renewed in sexual intercourse, when a man loses semen but,
paradoxically, gains some power which enables him to continue working. (3) It is perhaps to this gain that the word 'completarse' -
to complete oneself (which is given by men as their reason for attending the brothel) refers.

This gain in strength is thought by Peruvians to be related in
some way to the physical health, the fatness of the women concerned.
A woman judged better-looking than many of her colleagues by an
American was rejected by the Peruvian workers as being too thin.
In the oil camps the situation is an extreme of that which exists
more generally. Men need the sexual women they have banned from
their homes, and this need is recognised by the women of the family,
who expect, or even require, men to indulge themselves sexually
outside the purity of the home. The brothel is the institution
which fulfils this need, and is accepted by men and women alike in
this role. At least in the brothel the terrifying, sexual woman is
kept under some control.

The organisation of prostitution in Peru is complex, and reveals

many of the unspoken assumptions about men, women and sexuality. In
the brothel there are many rules about times of working and so on,
which are imposed by the provincial governments. Prostitution is
legal in Peru, and each province is able to regulate its precise
form in the way it sees fit. There is considerable variation in how
this is done. For instance, in the next city to the one I am describing, prostitution is legally outlawed and there are nightclubs
instead of brothels.

However, there is a clandestine trade in all areas. The girls
who work illegally are called 'mariposas' - butterflies - and their
continuing existence even where prostitution is legal makes it seem
that one important attraction of prostitution is the enjoyment of
illicit sexual pleasure.

In the city I know best there are two brothels which, if they are
full, contain about thirty prostitutes. One is within the city and
I was refused permission by the landlady to investigate this house.
The other complies with a new law which requires the brothels to be
located at a particular distance from the city. As the administrator (4) told me, this is a good thing, as no one hears what is
going on, people can 'wander about half-nude and it doesn't matter'.
There is a mutual protection of the bad woman and the good wife, who
are clearly divided socially and separated physically, which spares
them the shame and anger of facing oneanother. However, this means
that men have to make a journey of about half an hour by bus and
foot, or fifteen minutes by car, to reach the sexual women. The
inconvenience is tolerated because of the benefits of keeping sex
out of the home and even the city, and in its rightful place, which
seems to be a rural setting.

The girls take out their papers and become prostitutes after
differing experiences which they see as precipitating them into the
life. One told me she was seduced by her employer whose wife threw
her out of the house when it became clear that the maid was
pregnant, reproduction not being the aim of that particular sexual
relationship. This woman was well able to look after herself in a
quite unobtrusive way. She was supporting her children (two by the
time I knew her) and her mother, and saving to set herself up in
business as a shopkeeper when she retired, which she hoped to do in
a year or two. She seemed realistic and, I thought, was more likely
to succeed in her aims than many of the other girls who often
mentioned similar plans, but spent their earnings with élan, or at
times became too depressed to work. One woman told me she had been
tricked into signing her papers by a hotelkeeper who led her to
believe she was just signing a work contract for the hotel.
(Whether this was true or not, there was nothing physically to stop
her from leaving the business.)

Most of the women working there had children, some born before
they became prostitutes and others conceived while their mothers
were working. The need to support these children was the most
common reason given for entering and staying in the business. There
is no doubt that jobs for women, in which the earnings are as high,
are few and far between in Peru, and probably beyond the reach of
most of these women. But as several of them working previously - in
factories, beauty shops, and as secretaries and nurses - economics
do not provide a sufficient explanation for entering the profession.

In fact the older women did hint at other reasons, saying that once a woman was accustomed to so much money, and the freedom of the prostitute's life, it was difficult to leave and give up all those things. There is a great contrast with the lives of the respectable women of roughly similar social class and backgrounds, for the prostitute travels from town to town as the mood takes her, she travels with friends or on her own and has plenty of money (as much as a university lecturer in 1974) which she can spend as she wishes.

Many of the girls spend their money on men - as if they wish to reverse the usual economic order to avoid dependency themselves, and put someone else in that potentially humiliating position. (5) Often I was with the women when they did use their financial superiority to apparently turn the tables on men, treating the latter as children and buying them meals and presents. At other times I have been in restaurants with women from the house who have ordered the waiters around in an aggressive way - again reversing the usual situation of dependency of women upon men, and exploiting it to the full.

However, as if to counteract this economic power of the prostitute she is kept under the watchful eye of the State. She has to present herself and her papers to the bastions of male power represented by the police station and the hospital. A hospital visit is required every week, at which the girls are examined cursorily for signs of disease and given a large dose of penicillin anyway. Since this procedure is likely to be creating increasingly virulent strains of venereal disease it is most usefully understood as a ritual directed at psychic forces rather than a purely physical prophylactic measure. The penicillin is given as an injection. In Peru medicine is not believed to be particularly effective unless it is given in this way. This is especially interesting as sexual intercourse is sometimes referred to, in slang, as the man giving the woman an injection. Physical penetration allows the exchange of mystical, healing or impregnating powers.

The medical inspection and injection of the prostitutes takes place at 8.30 a.m. on Saturday morning, which is a very awkward time for women who work into the early hours of the morning, and whose hardest days are Friday and Saturday. The visit to the police takes place each Thursday afternoon when papers are inspected and stamped. The police know the girls' real names, and, in fact, have a great deal of power over the prostitutes.

This system of checks and controls ostensibly protects the women and their clients from disease, but also allows the men to follow and control the movements of the dangerous sexual woman. The same system isolates this woman from the respectable women of the city, but provides the prostitute with some protection. For instance, a woman has to run and own the house and this gives her power and wealth within society. The law also forbids pimping, to attempt to limit the prostitutes' exploitation, which nevertheless continues, but there is a protection for the prostitute in that the landlady can call the police to remove a man she suspects of pimping. There is a deep psychological need for these exploitative relationships between pimp and prostitute, and they flourish, women being threatened to extort money from them and so on, in spite of the possibility of legal protection offered by the State.

THE WOMEN OF THE BROTHEL

The reasons why the prostitutes do not avail themselves of the
possibility of legal protection brings us to another level of understanding of prostitution. As well as being seen as a terrifying
element of society which needs to be isolated and controlled, some
of the women seem to have internalised a view of themselves as bad,
to be degraded and exploited. The prostitute is full of self-doubts
and self-hatred. There are many illustrations of the fact that this
is so. The girls often have pimps, especially those women who are
not particularly competent and tough. These men are usually university students, well-dressed and good-looking, perhaps slightly
effeminately pretty. They only visit to take money from the girls,
if necessary with threats of violence. Other pimps may stay with
their girls for a longer time, but as this inevitably inhibits
business, it is not a particularly productive arrangement. Other
women are married and live with their husbands in the city, but they
tend to be older women who are about to leave the business and often
succeed in doing so. The marriages of the young women seem to fail
very frequently and they return to the business with yet another
child to support. On the whole the prostitute's relationship with
men, clients or otherwise, tends to be unsatisfactory and to reinforce the isolation from society which often begins when a woman
enters the profession and has to leave home and perhaps lie to her
family about what she is doing.
  Within the brothel the women also tend to be alone. They normally travel around Peru in pairs or singly. The pairs are at times
extremely close - they often spend the daytime in bed together - and
provide a means to survive their lonely existence. Prostitutes do
not allow or expect men to give them any lasting affection or
comfort, and get it rather from women. But the friendships between
women are fragile alliances, broken by quarrels over men, and behaviour such as bumping into one another on the dance floor. The
whole house erupts into continual quarrels and fights at times - as
the administrator told me in desperation 'gossip here, gossip there,
it is like hell'. If one woman is a 'trouble-maker' the arguments
can be continual - about money owed, and men. One of the favourite
insults is to call another girl a whore, and the daughter of a
whore. One woman told me that other girls or men try to cut your
face, and sometimes men scar your stomach. She was marked all over
her stomach and many women had scars on their faces. The administrator told me that the thing to do is put garlic under your finger-
nails before attacking someone and when the scratches heal they will
leave black scars. The administrator also described a fight about a
man which began in the night. One of the girls continued to drink
and in the morning was found with a knife cutting at her opponent's
forehead as she lay on the ground. As the administrator said, it
could just as easily have been the victim's throat. In such situations it is the elderly woman administrator who has to cope. The
men working in the house cannot be relied upon to deal with the
violence. Even at night, when she runs the bar, if there is trouble
she 'drops everything and runs for the police' who must be a mile
away, and there are no telephone lines. The brothel is an island of
tension and discord, not linked to the police or other agents of

social control available to the rest of society, and violence is
inevitably part of its activities.

It is not surpring that one of the toughest and most capable
women I met there told me that she had to put on her make-up hours
before she began to work as her hands shook so much. She at least
cared for herself enough in some ways to take contraceptive
measures. Many of the more depressed and less competent women took
no precautions whatsoever, and they would find themselves pregnant
frequently. One girl told me she did not take the pill (which is
readily available in Peru) as she was afraid of getting fat. I was
told that the cap was dangerous because there was a possibility of
getting cancer from the rubber, and I think it was little used.
Several of the girls were given three-monthly contraceptive in-
jections. Others would buy French Letters but did not, apparently,
always insist that the clients used them. Such gestures seem to me
to be an expression of how little they cared for themselves and how
hopeless life seemed to them. When they were pregnant they would
continue working, although this is illegal. One girl of about
eighteen was four or five months pregnant, but she told us she
held in her stomach and no one noticed at the medical inspection.
She disappeared a week or so later and we were told she had gone
home very ill after a miscarriage. The prostitutes themselves
refuse to protect themselves, or to make use of legislation passed
for their protection. No doubt they need to carry on working, but
they also seem to be bent on self-punishment and self-destruction,
acting in the way the myth that they are evil, sexual women seems
to require.

Another example of this self-neglect is the fact that the girls
are told to inspect the men for disease by stroking the penis and
looking for any discharge. Although it seems unlikely to afford any
real protection from VD, many girls preferred to risk the fact that
the man might be diseased, and to keep the lights low, so that the
men cannot see their bodies. There are such intense feelings of
shame attached to prostitution that they outweigh the desire to care
for the woman's own body and general health.

There are numerous other examples of the prostitute's low self-
esteem. One woman said her boyfriend was 'chinese', meaning he
looked unattractive, and it was just as well as otherwise he would
leave her. She took him many presents each time she went home and
was clearly enormously fond of him. He was much younger than she
was. She had left her first husband because she was 'hot' and he
was 'cold'. She described how she became extremely excited when a
man touched her breasts and seemed to enjoy sex. But she would
cover her face when making love and would not let clients kiss her
on the mouth. She was the only woman I met who gave credence to the
view that the prostitute is a more sexual person than her respectable counterpart. My impression is that most of the women regarded
sex as a job, and they would make a distinction between what they
felt with husbands or boyfriends and with clients.

Distrust and dislike of other women is more strongly expressed
in the brothel, but it is a theme which runs throughout the city.
Other girls will give you bad advice about your appearance, I was
told. Other women are stupid, not able to look after themselves.
Among the prostitutes who are isolated from society, and exist to

satisfy the sexual desires of men which are socially unacceptable, (6) such feelings reach a height so that violence is almost a relief.

THE SOCIAL SYSTEM OF THE BROTHEL

Alongside all this tension and destructiveness there are moral codes in the brothel to which the women are expected to adhere. On my second visit there a shrine had been built just outside the yard of the house because the girls wanted to burn candles, I was told, though I never saw it in use. A similar gesture - half mocking, half serious - perhaps cocking a snook - at conventional morality was made when several men who had just bought a bus wanted to take it to an important shrine in the mountains to be blessed. They invited several of the girls and myself to come along and we took lots of food and drink and had a riotous time, lighting candles and making a lot of noise. I have no idea if the priest realised who we were, but it seems that the prostitute, and the foreign anthropologist, can share this sort of gay outing, where a respectable Peruvian woman cannot.

There are also articulated standards by which prostitutes judge one another. Some girls are said to 'get up at dawn and screw with anyone' and are gossipped about and looked down upon. Others may spend much of their daytime leisure with men, which is again suspect and they are treated accordingly. For the hours during which it is accepted for women to attend to a man are rigidly defined - both formally and informally - as after seven o'clock and until the bar closes. This time varies according to the number of clients on a particular night. Such informal standards are backed up by the State which makes it illegal for men to stay overnight, perhaps in a further attempt to protect the client and the prostitute, and to make the distinction between the bad and good woman even more apparent. Women who frequently change their friendships within the brothel are also regarded as transgressing moral codes. So even within the brothel there is a split between the good and bad woman prostitute. Outside the brothel women do not acknowledge clients - once again the prostitute is isolated and her existence denied. The women often regard this as a protection for themselves because they are at least able to walk around the city anonymously, or relatively so. In smaller towns prostitutes are known and suffer such indignities as being forbidden to go to the cinema except in particular seats. The number of foreigners in the particular city I studied no doubt adds to their anonymity. In spite of this the administrator - who often acts as a mother/advisor, looking after the possessions of girls who are travelling elsewhere and so on - tells them 'not to show in the street what they are'. They are told to behave quietly and not draw attention to themselves. It is unseemly to act as many of them do - aggressively discussing their travels and economic independence in public places. This happens when a group of women goes into town. They are also ferociously independent and would not let me pay for any meals or drinks which we had together. The quieter women would prefer to take another bus, on their own, than to be mixed up with this aggressive display, although it is only too clear that one is visiting the brothel as there are no other buildings near the bus stop, which is known as 'the curve'. This means that sometimes the bus drivers regard it as amusing to refuse to stop to let the girls either mount or alight from the bus. This is not done to the men who visit, however. The administrator was very concerned about my visiting her by bus as people were bound to say 'bad things' about me. The barrier which exists between the brothel and the rest of society is still enormous - the owner of the house told me that only a foreigner would visit them, and she was very pleased that I did so. She also asked me one day if we had free love in England, and when I said no, and tried to explain, she said 'thank goodness for that'. Her own position in society is very confused - her sons are being educated at her expense all over the world, but she has to put up with anonymous, insulting phone calls being made to her house. The family feels itself to be the object of envy; for example, when a dog died mysteriously at the brothel, the owner's son told me it had had a spell put upon it by people who were jealous of their wealth. He chose to ignore entirely their dubious position in society and point to the undeniable and simple fact of their economic power.

There is another side to the view of the prostitute as a 'bad' woman, which receives a great deal of emphasis. I have described how women prefer their husbands to visit prostitutes, who do not represent a threat to their own marriages. The prostitute is accepted as someone who fulfils a necessary function and tolerates behaviour and aspects of men which are believed to be unacceptable to a wife. The prostitutes also subscribe to this view of themselves. I was repeatedly told that what mattered was not looks, clothes or other externals, but 'luck', which was sometimes defined as sex-appeal, and most important of all, knowing how to treat clients well. This was stressed all the time. Angry clients have to be soothed, sad clients comforted. One woman was so moved describing this situation that she was in tears herself - perhaps also with the knowledge that there was no one to fulfil that function for her. There is a saying that prostitutes make the best wives because they really know all the sides of men. Although this does not seem to work in practice, there is a strong desire to idealise the prostitute. Another woman told me that prostitution was a 'pillar of socialism', perhaps based on the principle of sharing. But the main element of this non-idealised view of prostitution was aptly described by the administrator, who said 'someone has to bear the kicks'. The prostitute tolerates and holds the intolerable and unbearable aggression, frustration and pain which convention requires be kept out of the home, and the relationship between husband and wife. It is to fulfil this crucial need that prostitution has always existed. The need is greater where men and women are forced to live up to expectations which they cannot realistically fulfil - a Peruvian 'mestizo' man is expected to be strong and decisive, a Peruvian 'mestiza' is supposed to be passive and submissive. The man is able to show his depression, weakness or frustration with life only to the prostitute. For the women the prostitute is like a lost part of herself which exerts a continual fascination for her - the 'bad' woman contains the 'good' woman's sexuality, strength and aggression.

THE EVENING AT THE BROTHEL - A JOURNEY INTO A PROFANE 'OTHER' REALM

'Callejon' is the first part of the evening. This means alleyway, and its name indicates the significance of the distinction drawn between women who are inside and outside the home. The women in the brothel stand in the doorways of their small rooms, while the men walk along the narrow alleyway between the wall of the central dance hall and the girls' rooms. Men arrive as darkness falls and 'callejon' lasts for about four hours. Prices are lower during this time. Later the women and their clients move into the centre of the brothel and the evening changes its character.

'Salon' begins at about eleven o'clock, and the women are reminded to leave their rooms and come into the central dance hall by one of the men working in the house. For this time they sometimes wear special clothes - short or transparent dresses, wigs and so on. The prostitutes seem reluctant to come in and it is soon apparent why. There are only a few men and they are drinking and talking to one another or the barlady. If they notice the women it is often only to make jokes at their expense. A woman who fears she will not earn enough otherwise may allow herself to be used in this way, and will dance with the different men as the juke box, or the band, starts to play. When I was there the women I knew came to talk and would then say they were now going to screw someone, or eat shit, and go and approach a potential customer. The atmosphere is one of underlying tension and hostility relieved by drink and jokes. Before going to the room, what the client wants and a price for it are discussed. Over the two years in which I knew the house, 'poses' became far more common. In fact I was told that men came for 'poses', which are any positions for sexual intercourse other than the missionary position, half-clothed, which seems to be usual in marriage. It is 'poses' which are of central importance, not only for the men but for the women. They are talked of with great shame, or a show of bravado. Women said that now 'poses' were required of them (though some women still refused to do them) the life was much harder to bear, and they had to rely increasingly on the effects of drinks and drugs to get through an evening's work.

The 'poses' seem to divide broadly into three types - one in which the woman is put into a position of humiliation, others in which the man puts himself beneath the woman, and those in which both partners indulge in activities which involve a greater intimacy than the intercourse of marriage. The prostitute and her client have a closeness in sex as in other ways which is not tolerable within marriage, due to the expectations of men and women which are normal in the provincial culture. (7) This is another reason why the prostitute is so isolated and controlled by society, even as she seems to be integral to it.

ORIGIN OF GOOD AND BAD MOTHER IMAGES: AN INTERPRETATION

The prostitute satisfies the desire inside any individual for someone who will do exactly what is wanted - the 'good' mother of the infant's imaginings. When the prostitute does this she becomes the 'golden-hearted whore' of much of the fiction about prosti-

tution. Like the mother, she tolerates and makes acceptable
feelings which are suspected of being intolerable and dangerous.

To understand the mechanisms which lie behind this process, it
is necessary to consider one particular model of the growth of the
human psyche.

The infant is a helpless being, totally dependent upon his
mother for physical and psychical care. When his mother is able
to give the care he needs - feeding, washing, understanding and
toleration for his nameless fears - she is experienced as an
extremely powerful, but loved person. She is the 'good mother'
the infant desires, and his experience of her gives the infant a
reservoir of positive feelings which he is able to draw on
throughout his life. The belief in a 'golden-hearted whore' is
one aspect of the search for the good mother in infancy. Viewed
from this perspective the prostitute is someone who tolerates
desires and feelings which are feared to be unacceptable to most
people, for instance the wives of the clients, who are thus protected by the prostitute, from the dangers believed to be part of
sexuality. In the brothel I have described, the owmen emphasised
the importance of treating the clients well, and saw a major part
of their required role as tolerating the tales of fear and despair
brought by the men.

The infant also sees his mother as so powerful that the fear of
engulfment by her is never far away, especially for a male child who
has to differentiate himself before he can develop his masculinity.
Thus women in general, and prostitutes in particular, are sometimes
portrayed as devouring and swallowing men. The total dependence of
the baby on the mother creates ambivalent feelings towards her, even
when she is able to care for him; when she is unable to do so
strong hostility may be generated in the baby.

When the infant is uncomfortable or frightened and the mother is
not there to soothe him, she is experienced as a present 'bad
mother', represented by all the misery he feels. The baby imagines
revenging himself upon this 'bad woman' by controlling her, or attacking her. As he becomes more aware of the world around him, he
notices that the bad mother is in fact the absence of mother, and
begins to suspect that she leaves him because of the elder siblings
around, or maybe in order to be with father and indulge in secret
excitement. In his mind mother is bad because she is absent and
absent because she is sexual. The baby shifts his view of mother -
from good, present and caring to bad, absent and sexual - with fa-
cility, an ability which is perpetuated in some men's views of women
throughout life.

Otto Weininger (1903) illustrates these rapidly alternating
views of women, who he believed were erotically voracious monsters:

One can scarcely believe that women have ever been really
different, and now the sensual element may well be stronger
than before, since an extraordinarily large element in the
feminist movement is only a transformation from motherhood to
prostitution; it is far more whore-emancipation than woman-
emancipation and certainly the chief result will be the predominance of the sluttish element in women. (8)

It seems that the fear of the sexually free woman is universal,

and that 'free women' has come to mean 'sexually free and
available'.

Peruvian men, like their brothers elsewhere, guard against the
danger of the free woman by containing the other women neatly in the
home. And if one escapes into prostitution she is still safely restricted by the law of the land. Individual unspoken fears which
derive their strength from the infantile situation are institutionalised and become the basis of morality. 'Defence systems against
anxiety are the stuff that culture's made of' (Roheim, 1943, p.81).

Controls of sexuality are to some degree directed at archaic
mental mechanisms, as well as towards physical and economic factors.
(9) This explains why some of the controls of prostitution, such as
the Peruvian medical inspection, take on a ritual quality. The same
archaic mechanisms play their part in many of our relationships, but
the intimate physical relationship with the prostitute is often
created to cater for needs which are not believed to belong to the
rational, adult world which we strive to live in. The central link
between prostitute and client is sexual excitement, and it is necessary to examine its creation.

R.J.Stoller has suggested that sexual excitement is almost inevitably based upon the satisfaction of a perversion, which he defines
as an expression of hostility between the two sexual partners, both
of whom are able to fulfil some fantasy of their own in the perverse
sexual activity. Perversion is defined by an attitude of mind,
rather than a particular activity. Perversions which are seen as
shameful and unacceptable by their creator, and yet have to be repeated, are likely to be taken to a prostitute and are likely to be
based upon strong hostility to the partner. This hostility is re-
ciprocated by the prostitute, whose fantasies are also satisfied by
her role in the transaction, and this goes some way to explaining
the widely-held belief that prostitutes are frigid or lesbians.
This frigidity may be a means to fulfil the fantasy of the whore.
(Stoller describes the activities of a male prostitute and con-
cludes: 'The hustler knows he is out for power; he recognises he
has an advantage over most of his customers, he is not excited as
they are' (1976, p.125).) The hostility of the perversion stems
from a need to dominate the partner, and this need derives from the
infant's fear and hatred of his dependency upon his mother.

Both partners in a perverse act feel themselves to reverse this
dependency and to triumph over their partner. The scope for such
mutually satisfactory beliefs is greatest when sex roles are rigidly
defined in society at large. Where men are expected to live up to
the ideals of 'machismo' - to be decisive and dominant - any hint of
a reversal of this social order creates intense, mixed, and to some
people, exciting feelings. The women required to take up a physically dominating sexual position is degraded in cultural terms by
being forced into an unfeminine, sexual role, which may, however,
fulfil her fantasies of triumphing over men. The man is able to
indulge his socially unacceptable desire to be submissive sexually,
safe in the knowledge that the woman he does this with is a social
outcast, unable to challenge his status and image outside the
brothel.

The woman put into a sexual position designed to humiliate her
may feel that the man's excitement at his triumph over her has in

fact given her the upper hand. Prostitution fulfils an apparently universal need for illicit, fantasy-filled sexual experience, which must be gained outside the family and other institutions which are being attacked or undermined in fantasy. The prostitute is punished for her part in these attacks by those respectable members of society who are trying to control the desires her presence advertises.

In Peru male and female behaviours are more clearly defined and separated than in our own culture and the image of the prostitute emerges more clearly. It is recognised that prostitution allows society, and particularly the family, to exist by containing the attacks directed at these institutions. The individual needs satisfied by prostitution vary from person to person, but for society, prostitution provides one way of coming close to drawing aside the veil the sexes tacitly agree to draw between themselves.

NOTES

1 Much of the field material upon which this article is based was collected with Dr George Primov, and I am very grateful for his generosity in allowing me to use this material.

2 Trade is an activity which, in many parts of the world, is associated with prostitution, and this again emphasises how thin the dividing line between economic independence and prostitution is believed to be.

3 Bullough, quoting Van Gulik, describes a similar system of belief in ancient China, where the emperor would make love to as many women as possible, bringing them to a climax, but avoiding orgasm himself. In this way he was believed to absorb the 'yin' which women had in limitless supply, and this was believed to increase his own virility.

4 The landlady owns and organises the brothel in its relations with the outside world. The administrator - an elderly woman - lives in the house and is responsible for the day-to-day running of the establishment. She is in close contact with the prostitutes who work there. There are also women employed as cooks, and men who work as cleaners and waiters.

5 Kate Millett spoke to two prostitutes, both of whom emphasised that screwing for money is safer from an emotional point of view than doing it for affection. The fear of losing someone cared for is too great for women who fear a 'terrible emotional dependency' which one of the women describes as typical of the prostitute. Both prostitute and client circle around total dependency which is attacked, sought and denied.

6 The homosexual desires of men are also acceptable within the brothel. Homosexual men often visit, as they enjoy the atmosphere.

7 Roheim says 'that the sexual practices of a people are indeed prototypical and that from their position in coitus their whole psychic attitude may be inferred' (1932, p.221). In the city I am describing the brothel was apparently the only place where desires for poses could be satisfied. In the capital city the situation was very different - 'poses' were a part of many

sexual relationships within marriage. It seems probable that
these differences in sexual practice may relate to great differences in the culture of various cities within the same country.

8 Winick has conducted a very interesting survey of prostitutes'
clients' perceptions of the prostitutes and themselves. In
open-ended interviews American clients described why they went
to prostitutes - 73 per cent said 'because she gives me what I
want', 71 per cent thought it was colourful and interesting,
63 per cent for the negative mother image of the prostitute,
56 per cent because they liked the idea of the money going to
the pimp. Around 50 per cent mentioned the possibility that the
prostitute might fall in love with them and therefore leave the
business. Only 20-30 per cent mentioned the lack of responsibility, or impotence with others. The four most important
reasons mentioned hint at the underlying fantasies involved - a
woman who will really supply what is needed, which is in
contrast to the actual mother who is attacked in fantasy, and a
woman who is, in fact, supporting, perhaps dominating, the
pimp/father. These same men described their mothers and wives
as people who could take, but not give, and who needed to
control their menfolk. The clients described the pleasure they
got from being in control, sometimes to the extent of refraining
from sexual intercourse and thus showing that women were not
worth it. The prostitute must at times stand for a hated mother
who is to be controlled and degraded.

Another important factor for the clients was the empathy with
the prostitute, who was seen as a passive vessel whose wants
would be filled. Three quarters of the men described this sort
of feeling of passive expectation, like an infant with his
mother. The attraction of the image of the pimp was said to be
that he was supported by the prostitute and was like a boy
again, a sort of older brother to the infant/client. There is,
in fact, no risk of a father around - just older brothers who
share the same needs and dependency upon the mother. Dependency
is another crucial element in the prostitute/client relationship. In fantasy the client gives himself up to the prostitute,
but in reality he simply pays for her time. The prostitute can
also avoid dependency which she may fear.

9 'Sexual craving, which might seem, if anything, to be wholly determined by a periodic sexual need, is in large measure a
craving for reassurance to counteract the unconscious and
irrational terrors both of persecution and loss' (Money-Kyrle,
1939, p.141).

BIBLIOGRAPHY

ACTON, W. (1870), 'Prostitution', London.
BULLOUGH, V.L. (1964), 'The History of Prostitution', University
Books, New York.
GREENWALD, H. (1970), 'The Elegant Prostitute', Walker, New York.
HAYS, H.R. (1966), 'The Dangerous Sex', Pocket Books, New York.
MILLETT, K. (1975), 'The Prostitution Papers', Paladin, London.
MONEY-KYRLE, R.E. (1939), 'Superstition and Society', Hogarth Press,
London.

PAZ, O. (1961), 'The Labyrinth of Solitude', Grove Press, New York.
ROHEIM, G. (1932), The National Character of the Somali, 'International Journal of Psychoanalysis', 13, pp.199-221.
ROHEIM, G. (1943), The Origin and Function of Culture, 'Nervous and Mental Disease Monographs', no.69.
STOLLER, R.J. (1976), 'Perversion - the Erotic Form of Hatred', Harvester Press, Hassocks.
WEININGER, O. (1903), 'Geschlecht und Charakter', Leipzig.
WINICK, C. (1962), Prostitute's Clients' Perceptions of the Prostitutes and Themselves, 'International Journal of Social Psychiatry', 8, pp.289-97.
WINICK, C. and KINSIE, P.M. (1971), 'The Lively Commerce', Quadrangle Books, Chicago.

Part two

Representations of Women

THE PURE WOMAN

The nineteenth-century literary insistence on female 'purity' epitomizes the desexualization of the good woman. Thomas Hardy's creation of Tess and his struggle to give her acceptable form exemplifies the cost of this image of purity, for much of the original vitality of the woman he portrays is lost with the denial of her sexuality. Hardy's revisions are of great interest because of what they tell us about late Victorian attitudes to sexual morality in general and female sexuality in particular.

Chapter 4

Tess: The Making of a Pure Woman

Mary Jacobus

ACKNOWLEDGMENTS

I am grateful to the Trustees of the Thomas Hardy Memorial
Collection for permission to quote from the manuscript of 'Tess of
the d'Urbervilles' and to the Dorset Natural History and Archaeo-
logical Society for permission to quote from manuscript material
deposited in the Dorset County Museum, as well as to the staff of
the British Museum and of the Dorset County Museum. A version of
this essay appeared in 'Essays in Criticism', xxvi (October 1976),
and is reprinted here by permission of the editors.

PURITY AND CENSORSHIP

Havelock Ellis, while proclaiming the modernity of Hardy's treatment
of sexual questions in 'Jude the Obscure', had an important reser-
vation about 'Tess of the d'Urbervilles' (1891):

> I was repelled at the outset by the sub-title. It so happens
> that I have always regarded the conception of <u>purity</u>, when used
> in moral discussions, as a conception sadly in need of analysis.
> ... It seems to me doubtful whether anyone is entitled to use
> the word 'pure' without first defining precisely what he means,
> and still more doubtful whether an artist is called upon to
> define it at all, even in several hundred pages. I can quite
> conceive that the artist should take pleasure in the fact that
> his own creative revelation of life poured contempt on many old
> prejudices. But such an effect is neither powerful nor legiti-
> mate unless it is engrained in the texture of the narrative; it
> cannot be stuck on by a label. To me that glaring sub-title
> meant nothing, and I could not see what it should mean to
> Mr Hardy. (1)

The label, Hardy tells us, was added at the last moment, as 'the
estimate left in a candid mind of the heroine's character' (1912
Preface). It caused trouble from the start. To those who accept a
Christian definition of purity, it's preposterous; and to those who
don't, irrelevant. The difficulty in both cases is the same - that

77

of regarding Tess as somehow immune to the experience she undergoes.
To invoke purity in connection with a career that includes not
simply seduction, but collapse into kept woman and murderess, taxes
the linguistic resources of the most permissive conventional moral-
ist; as the formidable Mrs Oliphant put it, in a review which
epitomises the moral opposition aroused by 'Tess'; 'here the elaborate and indignant plea for Vice, that it is really Virtue, breaks
down altogether'. (2) On the other hand, to regard Tess as unimpli-
cated is to deny her the right of participation in her own life.
Robbed of responsibility, she is deprived of tragic status - reduced
throughout to the victim she does indeed become. Worst of all, she
is stripped of the sexual autonomy and the capacity for independent
being and doing which are among the most striking features of
Hardy's conception.

Hardy himself makes things worse by seeming to adopt the argument
for a split between act and intention - Angel Clare comes to realise
that 'The beauty of a character lay not in its achievements, but in
its aims and impulses; the true record lay not among things done,
but among things conceived' (f.488, p.388). (3) Yet Angel's response to Tess at the end of the novel is remarkable precisely
because he no longer makes this distinction but - knowing her a
murderess - accepts her as she is. Alternatively, it could be
argued that the terminology of conventional Christian morality is
ironically misapplied in order to reveal its inadequacy and
challenge the narrow Pauline definition of purity-as-abstinence
originally held by Angel. But however one interprets the label, the
real problem - as Havelock Ellis points out - is Hardy's failure to
'engrain' its implications in the texture of the narrative. In the
circumstances, it is illuminating to discover that Tess's purity is
a literary construct, 'stuck on' in retrospect like the sub-title to
meet objections which the novel had encountered even before its
publication in 1891. In Candour in English Fiction, a symposium on
the censorship question published in the 'New Review' for January
1890, Hardy had protested at the tyranny exercised over the novelist
by the conditions of magazine publication. (4) Designed for
household reading, the family magazines necessarily failed (in
Hardy's words) to 'foster the growth of the novel which reflects and
reveals life'. In particular, a rigid set of taboos - designed to
protect 'the Young Person' (i.e. the young girl) - governed the
fictional treatment of sexual questions. Hardy's experience during
the previous months in trying to publish 'Tess' lies behind his
protest, and the compromises he was about to make must already have
been in his mind. Faced with the dilemma of 'bring(ing) down the
thunders of respectability upon his head' or of 'whip(ping) and
scourg(ing his) characters into doing something contrary to their
natures', he writes of seeing no alternative but to

do despite to his best imaginative instincts by arranging a
dénouement which he knows to be indescribably unreal and mere-
tricious, but dear to the Grundyist and subscriber. If the true
artist ever weeps it probably is then, when he first discovers
the fearful price that he has to pay for the privilege of writing
in the English language - no less a price than the complete extinction, in the mind of every mature and penetrating reader, of
sympathetic belief in his personages. (5)

In the autumn of 1889, three successive rejections of the half-completed 'Tess' had shown Hardy the price he had to pay, if not for writing in the English language, at any rate for serial publication. Ironically, the very changes he made to placate 'the Grundyist and subscriber' produced anomalies which the conventional moralists were quick to seize on when the novel finally appeared.

The form of Hardy's compromise is implicit in his defiant subtitle. But its effects were much more far-reaching. Hardy's own account misleadingly suggests that his solution was a cynical and temporary bowdlerisation for the purposes of serial publication only. (6) In reality he also made lasting modifications to his original conception in an attempt to argue a case whose terms were dictated by the conventional moralists themselves. The attempt profoundly shaped the novel we read today, producing alterations in structure, plot, and characterisation which undermined his fictional argument as well as strengthening it - or rather, since Hardy himself said of 'Tess' that 'a novel is an impression, not an argument' (1892 Preface), substantially distorted its final impression. As the novel first stood, it was not only simpler in outline, but different in emphasis. A letter to Hardy's American publisher in 1889 merely states that the 'personal character and adventures' of his nobly-descended milkmaid are 'the immediate source of such interest as the tale may have', and notes that 'her position is based on fact', but there is no hint of polemic. (7) From the manuscript one can reconstruct the main features of the Ur-'Tess' - already comprising Tess's seduction, the birth and death of her child, Sorrow, and her courtship by Angel, breaking off with their marriage and Angel's wedding-night confession. All the events which make up the second half of the novel (Angel's departure, Tess's solitary ordeal, Alec's reappearance, the murder, and finally, the reunion of Tess and Angel before her death) belong to the later, post-1889 phase of composition. More baldly than the revised version, the Ur-'Tess' had dealt with the common-enough situation of a country girl seduced by her employer on first going into service. Her social, economic, and sexual vulnerability are unequivocally defined. Tess's original name, 'Love' (modified successively to Cis, Sue, and Rose-Mary before becoming Tess), suggests that Hardy always had in mind the crudely polarised attitudes to female sexuality embodied in Alec d'Urberville and Angel Clare (sexual possession versus idealisation). But there is evidence that the oppositions were at this stage less clear-cut, more realistically blurred, and more humanely conceived, than they later became. The original novel was not only less polemical, but elegiacally explored the recurrent Hardian theme implied by its original title, 'Too Late, Beloved!' This was to be a tragedy of thwarted potential in which unfulfilment expressed not only social and cultural ironies, but the irony of life itself.

Throughout his career Hardy was acutely sensitive to adverse criticism, and the grounds given for its refusal by the three magazines to which 'Tess' was offered bear significantly on its reshaping. Hardy had promised the novel to Tillotson's, a newspaper syndicate, but it was only when the portion up to and including the death of Sorrow was already in proof that they read it. Their immediate demand for major changes and deletions led Hardy to try his

luck elsewhere. (8) Edward Arnold, the editor of 'Murray's Magazine', wrote a friendly, regretful, but firm refusal based on his
decision not to publish what he called 'stories where the plot involves frequent and detailed reference to immoral situations'.
Arnold explicitly takes his stand on the opposite side of a contemporary debate to which Hardy himself was to contribute in another
'New Review' symposium, The Tree of Knowledge (1894), this time
about sex education for women:

> I know well enough (writes Arnold) that these tragedies are being
> played out every day in our midst, but I believe the less pub-
> licity they have the better, and that it is quite possible and
> very desirable for women to grow up and pass through life without
> the knowledge of them. (9)

In this version of the double standard, middle- and upper-class
women are to be sheltered from knowing what men of the same class
get up to with working-class women. But it was the third and last
rejection of 'Tess' that proved most decisive for its development.
It must also have been most wounding, based as it was not on an ob-
jection of principle, but on specific objections to Hardy's
treatment of his subject. Mowbray Morris, the editor of
'Macmillan's Magazine' - later to reply to Candour in English
Fiction with an editorial of his own (10) - reacted sharply to the
frankness with which Hardy had made Tess's seduction the central
feature of his novel:

> It is obvious from the first page what is to be Tess's fate at
> Trantridge; it is apparently obvious also to the mother, who
> does not seem to mind, consoling herself with the somewhat cyni-
> cal reflection that she may be made a lady after if not before.
> All the first part therefore is a sort of prologue to the girl's
> seduction which is hardly ever, and can hardly ever be out of the
> reader's mind.

He goes on to reveal particular unease about the prominence given to
Tess's sexuality, both in its own right and in its effect on others:

> Even Angel Clare (he complains) ... has not as yet got beyond a
> purely sensuous admiration for her person. Tess herself does not
> appear to have any feelings of this sort about her; but her
> capacity for stirring and by implication for gratifying these
> feelings for others is pressed rather more frequently and elabo-
> rately than strikes me as altogether convenient ... You use the
> word succulent more than once to describe the general appearance
> and condition of the Frome Valley. Perhaps I might say that the
> general impression left on me by reading your story ... is one
> of rather too much succulence. (11)

Morris's prejudices - against women capable of sexual arousal as
well as of arousing others - are revealing in themselves; in an
anonymous and hostile review of the novel as it finally appeared,
he was again to accuse Hardy of tastelessly parading what he calls
his heroine's 'sensual qualifications for the part'. (12) It is in
the light of such reactions that Hardy's purification of Tess must
be seen. The changes he made tell us not only about the strains
which underlie one of his greatest novels, but about late Victorian
attitudes to female sexuality.

REHABILITATION

Hardy's reply to Arnold is summed up in the words of the 'Explana-
tory Note' to the first edition: 'If an offence come out of the
truth, better is it that the offence come than that the truth be
concealed' (p.27). His reply to Morris is contained in his sub-
title. A sustained campaign of rehabilitation makes Tess's so
blatant a case of the double standard of sexual morality applied to
men and women, and Tess herself so blameless, that the tragedy of
the ordinary becomes the tragedy of the exceptional - blackening
both man and fate in the process. In Hardy's original scheme, Tess
becomes exceptional precisely through the experience she undergoes.
She starts as a village girl distinguished from others only by her
freshness, her ancestry, and the fecklessness of her parents. The
gap between herself and her mother seems less great and, important-
ly, she has known of her pedigree 'ever since her infancy' (f.141*).
In the revised version, however, 'Sir John' first learns of his
lineage in the opening scene of the book. Hardy's intention in
making this change is obviously to play down the inevitability of
which Morris complained. (13) Originally, her seduction had sprung
from a realistic combination of circumstances - her mother's simple-
mindedness (seeing Alec's attentions as Tess's chance to marry a
gentleman), her father's irresponsibility (getting too drunk to
drive the loaded cart to market, and hence throwing on Tess the
guilt of Prince's death), and her own inexperience. In the revised
manuscript, her entire tragedy springs from this opening encounter
with an antiquarian parson, and can now be blamed on a peculiarly
malign chain of events. With this development of the heroine's
ancestry into the main-spring of her tragedy goes the endowing of
Tess herself with special qualities of dignity and refinement.
Mrs Oliphant calls it 'a pardonable extravagance' in a partizan
author to make her 'a kind of princess' in her village milieu. (14)
But is it? Later in the novel, Angel Clare recognises that the
consciousness on which he has intruded is Tess's single opportunity
of existence - that she is 'a woman, who at her lowest estimate as
an ordinary mortal had a life which, to herself who endured or
enjoyed it, possessed as great a dimension and importance as the
life of the mightiest to him'(f.218*, p.195). Though we see Tess as
one anonymous field-woman among others, harvesting at Marlott or
turnip-hacking at Flintcombe-Ash, her inner world is unique. (15)
To make her tragedy inseparable from her distinction is to belie the
humane and egalitarian impulse at the heart of the novel - its assertion of the value of any individual, however commonplace, however
obscure.

To give Tess from the start a privileged sensibility - make her
especially conscious of her parents' shortcomings, especially responsible, especially alert to the implications of Alec's behaviour
- also works against a central motif in the Ur-'Tess': that of
growth through experience. Hardy's conception of character is an
organic one. He starts with an unformed heroine, and shows us the
emergence of a reflective consciousness close to his own. Tess's
'corporeal blight had been her mental harvest' (f.176*, p.163), he
observes; the seduction and its aftermath leave her with a sombre
sense of personal insignificance and vulnerability. In her own

language she expresses what Hardy calls 'the spirit of modernism' (f.176*, p.163), the uncertainty of life without a benign providence or an assured future:

> 'you see numbers of to-morrows just all in a line, the first of them the biggest and clearest, the others getting smaller and smaller as they stand further away; but they all seem very fierce and cruel, and as if they said, "Beware o' me! Beware o' me!"' (f.175*, p.163)

In this respect, 'Tess' - like so many of Hardy's novels - concerns education. The actuality and the metaphor of journeying pervade the novel, reflecting both Tess's changing circumstances, and, most movingly, her capacity for endurance. In a particularly interesting passage Hardy extends the metaphor to embrace education through experience, drawing on a quotation from Ascham's 'Schoolmaster': '"By experience", says Roger Ascham, "we find out a short way by a long wandering." Not seldom that long wandering unfits us for further travel, and of what use is our experience to us then?' (f.135*, p.134). The context of Ascham's remark had been a criticism of experience as a mode of teaching:

> Learning teacheth more in one year than experience in twenty, and learning teacheth safely, when experience maketh more miserable than wise. He hazardeth sore that waxeth wise by experience ... We know by experience itself that it is a marvelous pain to find out but a short way by long wandering. (16)

Wise fathers, he continues, teach their children rather than committing them to the school of life - an injunction picked up when Tess turns on her mother with the lament, '"Why didn't you tell me there was danger? Why didn't you warn me?"' (f.111*, p.117). (17)

 A necessary consequence of Hardy's campaign to purify Tess is the character-assassination of Alec and Angel. Hardy's remark that, 'but for the world's opinion', her seduction would have been counted 'rather a liberal education to her than otherwise' (f.136*, p.135) was always sweeping in view of its result, Sorrow. But it makes more sense in the context of the relationship with Alec as originally envisaged. At this stage Alec had been younger (21 or 22 rather than 23 or 24) and without the later element of fraud. Instead of being a spurious d'Urberville, a nouveau-riche with a stolen name, he is simply a yeoman-farmer called Hawnferne. Traces of this less hardened character live on in the episode - not present, of course, in the original version - in which Tess goes to claim kin at the Slopes and first meets Alec. We are told that 'a sooty fur represented for the present the dense black moustache that was to be' (ff.44-5; by the first edition, in 1891, it has grown to 'a well-groomed black moustache with curled points', p.68); although in training for the role, he is not yet the moustachioed seducer of Victorian melodrama. Present from the start, however, is the motif of sexual dominance expressed through mechanical power. In the opening pages of the Ur-'Tess', Alec has seen Tess at the club-walking and called on her mother; as she drives along in the small hours of the next morning, Tess's last thoughts before dropping off and waking to find Prince impaled by the on-coming mail-coach are of the young man 'whose gig was part of his body' (f.34*). Alec's gig - here tellingly juxtaposed with the death of Prince - is not simply the equivalent of a sports-car, his badge of machismo, wealth and

social status. It is also a symbolic expression of the way in which
Tess is to be deprived of control over her own body, whether by Alec
himself or by the alien rhythms of the threshing-machine at
Flintcombe-Ash, in a scene where sexual and economic oppression are
as closely identified as they had been in her seduction.

The gig motif makes the nature of Alec's power over Tess particularly explicit. But it also provides scope for the rough and tumble
of a more robustly-conceived situation in their two most important
scenes together, the drive to the Slopes and - in the Ur-'Tess' -
the night of the seduction itself. It is in these scenes that the
effect of Hardy's later modifications to the character of Tess
emerges most clearly. The drive to the Slopes, Tess's first real
encounter with Alec, shows her confused but sturdy in the face of
his sexual bullying; above all, it shows her as less conscious.
After being forced to clasp his waist during one of the pell-mell
down-hill gallops contrived by Alec for the purpose, the original
Tess exclaims '"Safe thank God!" ... with a sigh of relief'; the
later, more aware Tess adds '"in spite of your folly!" ... her face
on fire' (f.65*, p.84). In the same way, after her ruse to get out
of the gig (letting her hat blow off), she refuses to get up again
with '"No Sir", she said, firmly and smiling' - whereas the later,
more sophisticated Tess reveals 'the red and ivory of her mouth in
defiant triumph' (f.67*, p.86). The original relationship is thus
both more straightforward and more intimate. Just before the seduction itself, Hardy comments in the manuscript version that 'a
familiarity with his presence, which (Alec) had carefully cultivated
in (Tess) had removed all her original shyness of him' (f.92*, pp.
103-4); (18) and we see this familiarity in the earlier version of
the scene in which Alec gives her a whistling lesson. Tess purses
her lips as he instructs, 'laughing however' (revised to 'laughing
distressfully however', f.75*, p.92), and when she produces a note
'the momentary pleasure of success got the better of her; and she
involuntarily smiled in his face like a child' (f.75*, p.92) - the
last phrase deleted from the revised version. This more naive and
trusting Tess figures in the prelude to her seduction, the orgi-
astic Trantridge dance. As she looks on, waiting for company on her
homeward walk, Alec appears; and we see her confiding her problem
to him, declining his offer of a lift warily ('"I am much obliged to
'ee, sir", she answered') but without the formality of the later
version - '"I am much obliged", she answered frigidly' (f.85*, p.98)
- where she has become the alert repulser of his attentions. The
suggestion of greater intimacy is picked up in a conversation later
that night, after Alec has rescued Tess from the Amazonian sisters
who pick a quarrel with her on the way home:

'(Tess), how many times have I kissed you since you have been
here?'
'You know as well as I.'
'Not many.'
'Too many.'
'Only about four times, and never once on the lips, because you
turn away so.' (f.92*, p.103) (19)

This is inconveniently explicit in the context of a purified Tess,
and it is deleted altogether from the later version. But it reflects the greater degree of intimacy permitted by the Ur-'Tess'
which in turn makes the seduction itself credible.

'The girl who escapes from her fellow-servants in their jollity
by jumping up on horseback ... behind a master of such a character,
and being carried off by him in the middle of the night, naturally
leaves her reputation behind her.' (20) Mrs Oliphant's absurd
verdict is unexpectedly pertinent to the revised version. But the
problem doesn't arise in the Ur-'Tess'. Once again the gig - the
more prosaic but more probable means of Tess's rescue in the original version - plays an important part in this crucial scene. In the
later version, Tess reacts to Alec's attempt to put his arm round
her by a little push that threatens to make him lose his balance,
perched sideways on his horse with her behind him. In the Ur-
'Tess', however, she reacts with an unlady-like vigour which makes
him fall right out of the gig and onto the ground, winding him in
the process. Alec makes the most of his fall, capitalising on her
genuine alarm and penitence - '"O I am so sorry, Mr Hawnferne! have
I hurt you? Have I killed 'ee? Do speak to me!"' (f.94*, p.104) -
to renew his complaints about being kept at arm's length. (21) The
incident puts Tess firmly in the wrong, and makes her acquiesce in
driving on beside him with his arm round her ('"because I thought I
had wronged you by that push"', f.95*, p.105) until she realises
that they are nowhere near home. It is at this point that Hardy
introduces the motif of intoxication which printed versions omit
after 1891. Earlier, the death of Prince had been the direct result
of her father's drunkenness and Tess's exhaustion. Hawnferne's is
specifically described as a drinking farm, and the Trantridge dance,
with its stupefied couples falling to the ground, prepares for
Tess's own collapse in the Chase. She too is caught up in the
Trantridge ethos when she accepts Alec's offer of a warming draught
of spirits before he goes off to look for the road. The logic of
the scenario - confused, realistically mingling accident and design,
character and situation - is entirely convincing. When Tess looks
back on the events leading up to her fall, she reflects accurately
enough: 'She had never cared for him, she did not care for him now.
She had dreaded him, winced at him, succumbed to him, and that was
all' (f.111*, p.117). In 1892 Hardy accentuated Alec's role as
seducer by adding 'succumbed to a cruel advantage he took of her
helplessness'. But it needed more than this to transform seduction
into the near-rape demanded by the purification of Tess, and at the
same time Hardy added the comments of the Marlott villagers as Tess
suckles her child in the harvest-field:

'A little more than persuading had to do wi' the coming o't....
There were they that heard a sobbing one night last year in The
Chase; and it mid ha' gone hard wi' a certain party if folks had
come along' (p.126).

Like Milton, Hardy has produced two versions of the fall - one,
comprehensible in human terms, the other retrospectively imposed for
the sake of his argument.

THE WAGES OF SIN

The aftermath of Tess's stay at the Slopes is explicitly post-
lapsarian; Tess has discovered that 'the serpent hisses where the
sweet birds sing' (f.102*, p.110), and she makes her exit from the

paradise of unknowing pursued by the text-painters' flaming letters:
'THE, WAGES, OF, SIN, IS, DEATH' (in the first edition, 'THY, DAMNA-
TION, SLUMBERETH, NOT', f.108*, p.114). Manuscript evidence
suggests that the period of Tess's dejection at Marlott originally
occupied a larger space, (22) which encourages the idea that Hardy
had wished to stress its part in bringing the mature Tess into
being. Paradoxically, it is her seduction that has made her a
fitting counterpart to the high-minded Angel Clare:

> At a leap almost (Tess) changed from simple girl to dignified
> woman. Symbols of reflectiveness passed into her face, and a
> note of tragedy at times into her voice. Her eyes grew larger
> and more eloquent. She became what would have been called a fine
> creature ... a woman whom the turbulent experiences of the last
> year or two had quite failed to demoralize. (f.136*, p.135)

Angel has been made reflective by thought as she has been by life -
talking the language of religious disaffection where she expresses
her sense of dissonance in the language of experience ('"there are
always more ladies than lords when you come to peel 'em"', f.178*,
p.165). Angel's dissent from the rigid fundamental Christianity of
his father, together with his harp-playing, single him out at once
as a thinking and a feeling man. The congruence of their sensibili-
ties is beautifully evoked in the overgrown garden where Tess has
been listening to Angel's playing. The garden perfectly expresses
the erotic potential of their relationship - potential coloured by
the implications of a fallen world. As she 'undulate(s) upon
(Angel's) notes as upon billows' (f.174*, p.162), Tess is surrounded
by a strange-smelling wilderness, 'damp and rank with succulent
grass and tall blooming weeds' (f.173*, p.161), in which snails
climb the stems of apple trees and sticky blights make blood-red
stains on Tess's skin. Melancholy and sensuousness are fused in the
highly-charged atmosphere of a June evening: 'The floating pollen
seemed to be his notes made visible, and the dampness of the garden
the tears of its sensibility' (f.174*, p.162). The same blend of
sensibility with the 'succulence' complained of by Morris (dutifully
revised to 'juicy') characterises their scenes of courtship in the
richly fertile Frome valley - scenes to which Hardy once again made
significant modifications.

Just as the purification of Tess had demanded the blackening of
Alec, it also required an increase in Angel's coldness and, as
before, in Tess's reticence. Like Alec, the original Angel had been
a younger and more believable character - bowled over by Tess,
perhaps against his better judgment, having had no thoughts of
marriage before. The early scenes between them are pervaded by
mutual sexual attraction which small but significant revisions
attempt to play down. For instance, when Tess archly accuses Angel
of ranging the cows to her advantage, her smile 'lifted her upper
lip gently in the middle so as to show three or four of her teeth,
while the lower remained still'; 'severely still' is the correction
(f.172*, p.161). Angel, burdened in one manuscript reading by a
'growing madness of passion ... for the seductive Tess' is less
overwhelmed in the final version by a 'waxing fervour of passion'
for a chastely 'soft and silent' Tess (f.210*, p.189). The crystal-
lising moment for both, their first embrace, is similarly censored.
When Angel comes impulsively round behind the cow Tess is milking

and takes her in his arms, the first version reads: '(Tess) yielded
to Angel's embrace as unreflectingly as a child. Having seen that
it was really her lover and no one else, her lips parted, she panted
in her impressionability, and burst into a succession of ecstatic
sobs' (f.214*, p.191). In the later version, Tess is more re-
strained: 'her lips parted, and she sank upon him in her momentary
joy, with something very like an ecstatic cry'. Angel has been on
the point of 'violently kissing' Tess's mouth, and declares himself
'passionately devoted' to her; we lose both the violence and the
passion, while Tess's emotion merely leads her to 'become agitated'
where before she had begun 'to sob in reality' (f.215*, p.192). As
Angel 'burns' to be with her, so Tess is permitted to be fully re-
sponsive; equally disturbed by their embrace, the two of them (not
just the Angel of the later version) keep apart - 'palpitating
bundles of nerves as both of them were' (f.216*, p.194). In so far
as they are distinguished at this stage, it is by a love that is
intellectual and imaginative on his side, and full of 'impassioned
warmth' on hers (f.292*, p.245). Angel is conceived, in contrast to
Alec, as a man in whom imagination and conscience are inseparable
from love; he wins Tess's 'tender respect' precisely by his
restraint (f.200*, p.180), and we are told that though he 'could
love intensely ... his love was more specifically of the solicitous
and cherishing mood' (ff.276-7*, p.234 - by 1891 it is a love 'in-
clined to the imaginative and ethereal'). Only in the post-1889
section of the novel do we hear of a love 'ethereal to a fault,
imaginative to impracticability' (f.349, p.287), of Angel's 'will to
subdue his physical emotion to his ideal emotion' (f.351, p.288) and
'his small compressed mouth' (f.335, p.277).

   The Angel of the Ur-'Tess' is scrupulous rather than obsessional.
Hardy has created an altogether more pitying portrait of a man who
cannot cope with the implications of the sexuality to which he none
the less responds - unconsciously preferring Tess spiritualised by
the light of dawn. Although he warms to the instinctual, easy-going
life of the dairy, he retains the morality of the vicarage. As Alec
is trapped by his own code of seduction and betrayal, so Angel was
to have been trapped by his puritan upbringing. We are told that
'despite his heterodox opinions' (changed in 1892 to 'heterodoxy,
faults, and weaknesses', f.218*, p.195), Angel never envisages sex
outside marriage. His acceptance of the ethical code practised by
his parents, despite his rejection of what he calls 'the miraculous'
element in Christianity, was to have been central to his tragedy.
It is in Angel's confession that Hardy's falsification of his
original intention can be seen most clearly. Angel's religious
dissent has been crucial, not only in preventing his entering the
Church like his brothers, but in preventing his going to university.
No less than Tess, he is socially displaced, and, in the eyes of his
family at least, damned for his views. The confession which he
embarks on in the Ur-'Tess' is quite simply one of unbelief:

   'Tess, have you noticed that though I am a parson's son, I don't
   go to church?'
   'I have - occasionally.'
   'Did you ever think why?'
   'I thought you did not like the parson of the parish.'
   'It was not that, for I don't know him. Didn't it strike you as

strange that being so mixed up with the church by family ties and traditions I have not entered it but have done the odd thing of learning to be a farmer?'

'It did once or twice, dear Angel.' (f.321*/2*) (23)

That the subject is clearly of more importance to Angel than Tess accentuates the intellectual gap between them. We cannot know how Angel would have continued, since at this point in the manuscript two pages have been condensed into one. A pencil draft for the final version, on the back of the surviving leaf, could suggest that Hardy had originally occupied the missing page with a much fuller statement of Angel's ethical position in the form of an extended quotation from St Paul (including an explicit denunciation of 'chambering and wantonness' as well as the more general injunction preserved in the final version: '"Be thou an example – in word, in conversation, in charity, in spirit, in faith, in purity"'; I Timothy 4.12, f.320/1, p.267). What is lacking is any indication whether Hardy had intended Angel to confess to a sexual episode in his own past paralleling Tess's. But although the Ur-'Tess' is disappointingly incomplete here, the clinching piece of evidence is provided by Hardy's earlier reference to this brief affair with an older woman, since it occurs on a new half-page pasted to an old one, onto which extra material has clearly been fitted (f.164*, pp. 154-5). The only reason for so substantial a revision would have been to make this earlier account of Angel's career square with a crucial change in his confession – a change motivated by Hardy's need to present a black and white case for Tess.

If Alec becomes an implausible villain, Angel, with his talk of purity, becomes a hypocritical proponent of the double standard. The overstatement does more than strain credibility – it falsifies Hardy's humane vision of individuals trapped by themselves and the ironies of their past. 'Too Late, Beloved!' takes on new force in the light of Tess's marriage to the man least able to overlook her deviation from Pauline ethics. That the virginal milkmaid of Angel's imagination is no longer 'pure' is as tragic for him as for her in the Ur-'Tess'. Significantly, it is only on their wedding-night in the original version that Angel learns of the decayed aristocratic descent to which he has slightingly referred on previous occasions (his unexpected pride in Tess's ancestry is an invention of the later version, where she confesses to it at an earlier stage). (24) Theirs had been tragedy of mutual incomprehension, almost, a collision of cultures as well as morals. The gulf between them is nowhere clearer than in Tess's original preparedness, before their marriage, to accept 'another kind of union with him, for his own sake, had he urged it upon her; that he might have retreated if discontented with her on learning her story' (f. 253*). Though less easy-going than her mother, Tess had been able to envisage an alternative to Angel's scrupulous morality. But such a thought is not allowed to cross the mind of a purified Tess; instead, the later version encumbers her with the naive and exonerating belief – displayed only after the confession (i.e. in the post-1889 phase of composition) – that Angel could divorce her if he wished. This high-minded heroine is not the same as the Tess of earlier scenes, torn between her desire to be honest with Angel and an understandable longing for happiness at all costs. With purifi-

cation comes inauthenticity and a new straining for effect in a
novel previously marked by its realism. Angel's rigidity, Tess's
humility, are equally forced; and it is surely significant that in
the scenes immediately following the confession – that is, in the
first scenes to be written when the novel was resumed after its successive rejections – Hardy's imagination should be seen to be
labouring under precisely the adverse conditions described by
Candour in English Fiction.

AFTERMATH

It would be wrong to imply that everything belonging to the later,
post-1889 phase of composition fell short of an earlier truth to
life. Tess's desolate period at Flintcombe-Ash is enough to show
Hardy's imagination functioning at its best, creating a universal
predicament out of individuals at work in a hostile landscape which
at once mirrors and dwarfs their suffering. All the same, Hardy
continued to modify his narrative even beyond this stage. Traces of
his original conception linger on especially in his handling of
Alec, whose reappearance initiates the final movement of the novel.
Predictably, Hardy superimposes the portrait of a fully-formed rake
on the Alec of the Trantridge period ('the aforetimed curves of
sensuousness', 'the lip-shapings that had meant seductiveness', 'the
bold prominent eye that had flashed upon her shrinking form in the
old time with such heartless and cruel grossness', f.439, p.352).
But the sincerity of Alec's conversion, and the genuine agony of his
loss of faith, are not questioned in the manuscript. There is irony
and factitiousness, but not hedonism or fraud. The Alec who can say
of his new-found faith, '"If you could only know, Tess, the sense of
security, the certainty that you can never fall away ..."' is ex-
pressing a religious sense deliberately dissipated by the text of
1902: '"If you could only know, Tess, the pleasure of having a good
slap at yourself"' (f.444, p.356). Tess's angry outburst first
meets with '"Tess ... don't speak so. It came to me like a shining
light"'; only in 1902, again, does this become '"It came to me like
a jolly new idea"' (f.444, p.356). When Alec reproaches himself for
'"the whole blackness of the sin, the awful, awful iniquity"'
(emended in 1902 to '"the whole unconventional business of our time
at Trantridge"', f.453, p.362), we may recoil from the crude
language of Christian condemnation, but it does not seem cynical.
The impression is of a man, however mistakenly, attempting to right
an old wrong in the terms laid down by his new morality, and made
wretched by the reawakening of sexual passion – coming to see Tess
with a marriage licence in his pocket, visiting her later when he
should be preaching to the 'poor sinners' (by 1902, 'poor drunken
boobies', f.464, p.371) who await him elsewhere, and leaving her
with the words, '"I'll go away – to hide – and – ah, can I! – pray"'
(secularised in 1902 to '"I'll go away – to swear – and – ah, can I!
mend"', f.464, p.371). Angel's had been an intellectual tragedy:
Alec's, a tragedy of passion. Ironically, it is Angel's arguments,
retailed by Tess, which lead Alec to lose the faith to which he had
been converted by Angel's father and which pave the way back to
Tess. Here Hardy's target is less Alec himself than the religious

doctrine which once more injures Tess in its failure to encompass the heterodoxy of human experience. (25)

Mrs Oliphant wrote indignantly of Tess's collapse, 'If Tess did this, then Tess ... was at twenty a much inferior creature to the unawakened Tess at sixteen who would not live upon the wages of iniquity.' (26) Exactly; Tess's suffering may deepen her, but it breaks her in the end. If the wages of sin is death, the wages of virtue - as we see at Flintcombe-Ash - are grinding poverty and back-breaking labour. As Tess puts it succinctly when Angel finds her living with Alec at Sandbourne, '"He bought me"' (by 1891, more reticently, '"He ---- "', f.539, p.429). Hardy's imaginative allegiance to Tess does not flinch from her subsequent act of murder - carried out with triumphant thoroughness in the earliest manuscript readings. The workman who finds Alec's body reports graphically '"He has been stabbed - the carving knife is sticking up in his heart"' (toned down to '"He has been hurt with the carving knife"', f.545, p.434), and Hardy himself underlines Tess's violence with 'The knife had been driven through the heart of the victim' (similarly toned down to 'The wound was small, but the point of the knife had touched the heart of the victim', f.545, p.343). Later, when Tess tells Angel of the murder, she does so with 'a triumphant smile' not 'a pitiful white smile'; '"I have done it well"', she claims, rather than the conventionally helpless '"I have done it - I don't know how"' (f.547, p.436). Hardy perhaps wished to play down Tess's unbalance for the sake of propriety, but his initial response to this imagined act is surely ours - that it repays the injustice to which Tess has been subjected throughout the book. Here, as elsewhere, Hardy's intuitive commitment was incompletely suppressed by the terms of reference imposed on him. Tess is not a woman to be admired for her purity or condemned for the lack of it; simply, she is a human being whose right to be is affirmed on every page, and whose death is the culminating injustice.

Mowbray Morris - to whom 'Tess' was 'a coarse and disagreeable story (told) in a coarse and disagreeable manner' (27) - summed up the proper purpose of fiction in his editorial reply to Candour in English Fiction: 'to console, to refresh, to amuse; to lighten the heavy and the weary weight, not to add to it; to distract, not to disturb.' (28) Hardy's own very different views were incorporated into the novel itself in the cancelled paragraph which originally introduced his final chapter and the hanging of Tess:

> The humble delineator of human character and human contingencies, whether his narrative deal with the actual or with the typical only, must primarily and above all things be sincere, however terrible sincerity may be. Gladly sometimes would such an one lie, for dear civility's sake, but for the ever-haunting afterthought, 'This work was not honest, and may do harm'. In typical history with all its liberty, there are, as in real history, features which can never be distorted with impunity and issues which should never be falsified. And perhaps in glancing at the misfortunes of such people as have or could have lived we may acquire some art in shielding from like misfortunes those who have yet to be born. If truth requires justification, surely this is an ample one. (f.563)

The question must be asked: did Hardy lie, if only 'for dear civility's sake'? Surely not. Though he chose to compromise in order to make his case and gain a hearing, he never falsified the issues. For all its blackening and whitewashing, the final version of 'Tess of the d'Urbervilles' is justified not only by its power to move and disturb, but by its essential truth.

NOTES

1   Concerning 'Jude the Obscure', 'Savoy Magazine', no.vi (October, 1896), p.40; reprinted in 'Thomas Hardy: The Critical Heritage', ed. R.G.Cox, London, Routledge & Kegan Paul, 1970. The difficulties raised by Hardy's sub-title are discussed by W.E.Davis, 'Tess of the d'Urbervilles': Some Ambiguities about a Pure Woman, 'Nineteenth Century Fiction', xxii (1968), pp. 397-401, and B.J.Paris, A Confusion of Many Standards: Conflicting Value Systems in 'Tess of the d'Urbervilles', 'Nineteenth Century Fiction', xxiv (1969), pp.57-79.

2   'Blackwood's Magazine', cli (March, 1892), p.473; reprinted in 'Thomas Hardy: The Critical Heritage', ed. R.G.Cox.

3   Page references in the text are to the New Wessex Edition, London, Macmillan, 1974. Folio references, in the case of quotations from manuscript, refer to the final pagination system adopted by Hardy in the manuscript preserved in the British Museum; asterisks denote leaves belonging to the earliest phase of composition. In quoting from ms., the text presented is that of the earliest readings, unless changes were clearly made at the same time; when quoting from revised passages, my text uses the latest readings. Ampersands have been silently expanded.

4   'New Review', ii (January, 1890), pp.15-21; reprinted in 'Thomas Hardy's Personal Writings', ed. H.Orel, London, Macmillan, 1967.

5   'New Review', ii, p.19.

6   See F.E.Hardy, 'The Early Life of Thomas Hardy', London, Macmillan, 1928, pp.290-1. Hardy's account is corrected by J.T.Laird in The Manuscript of Hardy's 'Tess of the d'Urbervilles' and what it tells us, 'Journal of the Australasian University Language and Literature Association', xxv (1966), pp.68-82, and, at greater length, in 'The Shaping of "Tess of the d'Urbervilles"', Oxford, Clarendon Press, 1975. My conclusions differ at times from Dr Laird's, but I have learned much from his exposition of the manuscript changes, and from Dr Juliet Grindle's valuable forthcoming Critical edition of 'Tess of the d'Urbervilles' (ms.D.Phil., Oxford, 1974), where a full account of the novel's evolution from ms. to the edition of 1912 is to be found.

7   4 August 1889, to J.R.Osgood; Pierpoint Morgan Library, quoted by Juliet Grindle, 'A Critical Edition of Thomas Hardy's "Tess of the d'Urbervilles"', p.viii.

8   See R.L.Purdy, 'Thomas Hardy: A Bibliographical Study', Oxford, Clarendon Press, 1954, pp.72-3. Hardy stood to gain 1,000 guineas from serial publication by Tillotson's.

9   15 November 1889; Dorset County Museum. See Michael Millgate, 'Thomas Hardy: His Career as a Novelist', London, Bodley Head,

1971, pp.283-4. Hardy's contribution to The Tree of Knowledge, 'New Review', x (June, 1894), pp.675-90, had stressed the importance of free access to knowledge, not only about sex in marriage, but about 'the possibilities which may lie in the past of the elect man' (p.681).

10   'Macmillan's Magazine', lxi (February, 1890), pp.314-20.

11   25 November 1889; Dorset County Museum. See Michael Millgate, 'Thomas Hardy: His Career as a Novelist', pp.284-6.

12   Culture and Anarchy, 'Quarterly Review', clxxiv (April, 1892), p.325; reprinted in full in 'Thomas Hardy: The Critical Heritage', ed. R.G.Cox.

13   See J.T.Laird, 'The Shaping of "Tess of the d'Urbervilles"', pp.109-17, for the development of the d'Urberville theme and its bearing on Hardy's portrayal of Tess as a victim of heredity.

14   'Blackwood's Magazine', cli, p.466.

15   Cf. Flora Thompson's description of individual field-women in 'Lark Rise to Candleford', World's Classics Edition, London, 1954, p.50: 'To a passer-by, seeing them bent over their work in a row, they might have appeared as alike as peas in a pod. They were not.'

16   'The Schoolmaster (1570)', ed. L.V.Ryan, Ithaca, N.Y., 1967, p.50.

17   Cf. not only Hardy's position in The Tree of Knowledge, but views apparently expressed to Edward Arnold, who wrote: 'I honour your motive which is, as you told me, to spare many girls the misery of unhappy marriages made in ignorance of how wicked men can be' (15 November 1889; Dorset County Museum. See Michael Millgate, 'Thomas Hardy: His Career as a Novelist', pp. 284-5). Later in the novel, Hardy made Alec complain that 'it is a sinful shame for parents to bring up their girls in such dangerous ignorance of the gins and nets that the wicked may set for them' (f.453, p.362).

18   The passage was moved backwards to its final place, after the whistling lesson (p.92), in the serial version.

19   Tess's name still stands as Sue, corrected to Rose-Mary, in this passage, which might indicate that it was deleted before the novel's rejection (by which time Tess had become the heroine's name).

20   'Blackwood's Magazine', cli, p.467.

21   In the Ur-'Tess', Alec complains that Tess has 'trifled with (his) feelings' for two months, not the three of the first edition.

22   There are three pages missing in the final foliation from the period between Tess's return home and her next appearance in the harvest-field after the birth of Sorrow, whereas eleven pages are missing from the Ur-'Tess' foliation.

23   The passage can be deciphered from the mirror-image on the verso; the second version is pasted over it on the recto.

24   Tess's 'substitute' confession of her ancestry, made in Chapter XXX, may originally have consisted of an account of her responsibility for the death of Prince; all that survives, however, is 'I - I - one night when my father was incapable, under' (f.268*).

25 Anti-religious protest seems originally to have been intended to
    play a larger part in the Ur-'Tess'; in a letter of 1 January
    1892 Hardy told Frederick Harrison that the first version had
    'said much more about religion as apart from theology', but that
    he 'thought it might do more harm than good and omitted the
    arguments, merely retaining the conclusions'; see Ann Bowden,
    The Thomas Hardy Collection, 'Library Chronicle of the Universi-
    ty of Texas', vii (1962), p.10.
26 'Blackwood's Magazine', cli, p.474.
27 'Quarterly Review', clxxiv, p.325.
28 'Macmillan's Magazine', lxi, p.319.

BIBLIOGRAPHY

J.T.LAIRD, 'The Shaping of "Tess of the d'Urbervilles"', Oxford,
Clarendon Press, 1975.
DAVID LODGE, Tess, Nature, and the Voices of Hardy, reprinted in
'Hardy: The Tragic Novels', ed. R.P.Draper, London, Macmillan,
1975.
TONY TANNER, Colour and Movement in 'Tess of the d'Urbervilles',
reprinted in 'Hardy: The Tragic Novels', ed. R.P.Draper.

THE AMAZON

Female warriors are considered an unnatural monstrosity or a mythic
ideal, since women are not commonly thought of as potentially feminine and also strong or able to create and defend their own culture.
The early Greek's version of the Amazon is revealed here as the
ideological construction of a pugnacious, paternalistic culture
whose nationalism required suitable enemies for their heroes.

Chapter 5

The City's Achievements

The patriotic Amazonamachy and
ancient Athens

Mandy Merck

> But it seems to me fitting that I should speak also of the city's
> achievements against the barbarians.... Now, while the most
> celebrated of our wars was the one against the Persians, yet
> certainly our deeds of old offer evidence no less strong for
> those who dispute over ancestral rights. For while Hellas was
> still insignificant, our territory was invaded by the Thracians,
> led by Eumolpus, son of Poseidon, and by the Scythians, led by
> the Amazons, the daughters of Ares.(Isocrates, 'Panegyricus',
> 65-8) (1)

ACKNOWLEDGMENTS

For invaluable information, theoretical discussion and bibliographical direction, my thanks to Mary Kelly, whose own work on this
subject I eagerly await. Also thanks to Susan Lipshitz and Barbara
Taylor for extensive help and encouragement, and to Jane Caplan,
Lindsay Cooper and Laura Mulvey for their useful comments.

As the Women's Movement debates its own cultural feminism, it seems
appropriate to reconsider that ideology's signal motif - the image
of the Amazon. Beneath the welter of contemporary mythographies
lies, as Adrienne Rich has recently observed, a valid purpose:
> Today, one quest of women is a search for models or blueprints of
> female power which shall be neither replications of male power
> nor carbon-copies of the male stereotype of the powerful, con-
> trolling destructive woman. The resurgence of interest in the
> work of J.J.Bachofen, Robert Briffault, Joseph Campbell, Robert
> Graves, Helen Diner, Jane Harrison, the response generated by
> E.G.Davis's 'The First Sex', has been in part a search for vindi-
> cation of the belief that patriarchy is in some ways a degener-
> ation, that women exerting power would use it differently from
> men: nonpossessively, nonviolently, nondestructively. (2)
A feminist history, a meditation on life unstructured by patriarchy, these are important, if not necessarily similar, projects.

But the Amazon myth stands at a stubborn distance from them, mediated by successive generations of analysis which have come to be conflated into the semblance of a single story.

Here Rich's bibliography is in itself revealing, combining as it does mythographies of very different purpose. Can we resort indiscriminately to a contemporary radical feminist like Davis ('Only the overthrow of the three-thousand-year-old beast of masculinist materialism will save the race' (3)) and a nineteenth-century evolutionary patriarchalist like Bachofen ('The triumph of paternity brings with it the liberation of the spirit from the manifestations of nature, a sublimation of human existence over the laws of material life' (4))?

If commentators as disparate as Davis and Bachofen have anything in common, it is literalism - their reading of myth as an actual record of the past. Shackled by the nineteenth century's fundamentalist antiquarianism, their inquiries fail to consider myth (whatever its connection to history) as ideology, and mythmaking as itself an historical event.

Davis prefaces the final chapter of 'The First Sex' with a citation from Edward Carpenter celebrating 'the new young women of today who, as the period of feminine enslavement passes away, send glances of recognition across the ages to their elder sisters'. If we take this as her, and our, purpose, we must be doubly wary of any uncritical appropriation of the Amazon myth. Across the ages our glance is met, not by our elder sisters, but their several images in a hall of distorting mirrors. The Amazon myth flourished, after all, in ancient Greece, particularly the state of Athens - a patriarchy which extensively mythologised women, but recorded first few - and then none - of their words, a culture distinguished both for its unusual degree of female subordination and its fascination with female dominance.

However feminists choose to recover the tradition, it seems essential to examine its first political uses. Contemporary commentators may argue for the actual existence of the warring tribes, or simply for the importance of the myth as a postulate of female power in antiquity. Neither view is politically adequate without an understanding of how the Greeks actually employed the image of 'the daughters of Ares'.

First, this essay considers the historical construction of the myth of the warrior women by the Greeks. The Amazons, I would argue, are not introduced into myth as an independent force, but as the vanquished opponents of heroes credited with the establishment and protection of the Athenian state, its founding fathers, so to speak. Patriotism reinforces patriarchalism to define the tribeswomen as opponents of the State, an image potent enough to be invoked by aspirant politicians.

Second, it locates the myth within the context of Athenian misogyny, where it may have functioned as a justification of that culture's radical subordination of women.

Finally, this essay questions the contemporary appropriation of the myth by feminists. Is the image of the warrior women severable from its originating context? Does it discourage or inspire our struggle against a constraining definition of femininity?

1   EARLY SOURCES

The earliest known references to the Amazons occur in the 'Iliad'.
Five times the warrior women, or one of their number, are named,
twice at some length: in Book 2 (lines 189 ff) Priam, the King of
Troy, recalls a youthful military campaign in Phrygia:
> and there I saw in multitudes the Phrygian warriors, masters of
> glancing steeds, even the peoples of Otreus and godlike Mygdon,
> that were then encamped along the banks of the Sangarius. For
> I, too, being their ally, was numbered among them on the day
> when the Amazons came, the peers of men....

In Book 6 (179 ff) they are named as one of the epochal foes killed
by the Greek hero Bellerophon:
> first he bade him slay the raging Chimaera. She was of divine
> stock, not of men, in the fore part a lion, in the hinder a
> serpent, and in the midst a goat, breathing forth in terrible
> wise the might of blazing fire. And Bellerophon slew her,
> trusting in the signs of the gods. Next fought he with the
> glorious Solymi, and this, said he, was the mightiest battle of
> warriors that ever he entered; and thirdly he slew the Amazons,
> women peers of men.

Here the Amazons already have a mythic status, peers not just of
men but of the great heroes, and a firm place in the epic catalogue
of legendary warriors. The oldest references are already allusive,
although in a sense this is true for all the matter of the early
epics, proceeding as they do from oral tradition. The problems of
their dating and authorship are immense, but it is generally agreed
that Homer, or whoever wrote the 'Iliad', must have lived before
700 BC (probably sometime in the eighth century), and that the
nearest approximation of the Troy of the poem is the archaeological-
ly-designated Troy VIIIa, which flourished for about 40 years before
its destruction by fire in the first half of the thirteenth century
BC.

This casts the historical basis of the 'Iliad' into the Mycenaean
Bronze Age, a civilisation which antedated that of Homer by half a
millennium. But Mycenaean Greece's relation to the later Iron Age
civilisation of the epics is extremely vague, not least because much
of its history and that of the intervening 'Dark Age', is unwritten.

Another suggested point of origin for the myth is the Hittite
civilisation, which dominated Asia Minor in the second millennium,
and came in contact with the Greek colonies in the eastern Aegean
around the twelfth century. There is a great deal of rather fanciful debate about whether the Amazons were really clean-shaven
Hittites, or whether their costumes in later vase-paintings include
items of Hittite apparel. (5) More interesting is Mina Zografou's
suggestion that the term 'Amazon' refers to a mixed-sex ethnic group
who lived in Asia Minor during the era of Hittite dominion
> what the Greeks considered as an Amazonic way of life and where
> the women fought in the wars ... the inexistence of the concept
> of marriage and fatherhood ... the custom of child-production
> through ritual promiscuity and ... the resistance ... to adopt
> the patriarchalistic customs that were brought and imposed by the
> peoples who placed Zeus at the head of the hierarchy of the gods
> detronizing (sic) the old Mother-Goddess. (6)

Unfortunately, Zografou's work at transliterating Homeric names and comparing them to contemporary Hittite records yields no more than a very speculative account of some possibly matrilineal Asian societies possibly involved in the political and ethnic upheavals which shook the thirteenth-century Aegean.

However, this essay does not purport to investigate the historical reality of the Amazon myth, but that of its application. In this I am encouraged by Martin Nilsson's observations on the subject:

It is uncertain what real fact underlies the myth of the race of warlike women, the Amazons. The opinion has been brought forward that they are a reminiscence of the Hittite empire, but that cannot be proved conclusively, though it may be possible. If this is so, the myths originated in the Mycenaean age. I am not able to make any decision, but I should like to observe that this myth was so famous it was sooner or làter applied to the most famous hero, Heracles. (7)

It is how the myth was 'sooner or later applied', its ideological uses in patriarchal society, which concern us here.

The next source for the Amazon myth is a post-Homeric epic by Arctinus of Miletus (eighth century BC). His 'Aethiopis' does not survive, but we know from a summary in Proclus' (AD 410 or 412-485) 'Literary Chrestomathia' (a handbook of classical Greek literature) that it was part of an eight-section Trojan cycle which included the 'Iliad' and the 'Odyssey'. (8) Proclus' work and other writings of post-Homeric and even post-classical authors, suggest a much broader body of sources than are available today. Even allowing for embellishments and plain inventions by later authors (and I will argue that these were extensive and often done with specific political motivations) the Amazon corpus seems to have been well-established, and available for allusion, by the eighth century. Gradually additional details were invented and/or written down, but most of what remains dates from long after the Homeric era, and is imbued with a sense of the subject's already mythical status.

The eighth-century 'Aethiopis' takes up the story of Troy after the killing of Hector by Achilles. Proclus' summary of the episode includes the arrival of the Amazon queen Penthesilea and her army from Thrace. This is already a departure from Homer (and an anomaly in the tradition generally, which tends to place the tribeswomen in the eastern or northeastern Aegean) and one historian suggests a political reason for this location: 'The change by Arktinos from Asia Minor to Thrace perhaps reflects increasing Ionian interest in the northern Aegean coasts and the Thraceward regions about 700 BC.' (9)

Penthesilea allies her army with the besieged Trojans, confronts the Acheans, and dies at the hands of Achilles. Photius' account simply says:

In the pride of her valour Achilles slays her, and the Trojans bury her. Achilles destroys Thersites for speaking slander against him and carping at his alleged love for Penthesilea; whence there is a division among the Greeks in regard to the murder of Thersites. (10)

2 THE HERACLES THEME

About the time of the 'Aethiopis', another Greek hero, one who shall
have even greater implications for the patriotic application of the
myth, joins Achilles and Bellerophon in the story. Much of the
Heracles myth is already present in the 'Iliad', but not his
conquest of the Amazons. It is in his 'Catalogue of Women' that we
find Hesiod (born sometime before 700 BC) referring briefly to

the mighty Herakles, when he was journeying in quest of the
horses of proud Laomedon - horses of the fleetest of foot that
the Asian land nourished - and destroyed in battle the tribe of
the dauntless Amazons and drove them forth from all that land.
(11)

This is the earliest available text of a story better known to us
in subsequent versions. (12) In it the heroic strongman, a son of
Zeus and the mortal Alcmene, is forced by Zeus' jealous wife Hera to
serve his elder cousin Eurystheus through a series of heroic deeds.
These twelve labours, the popular subject of legend and art, include
a voyage to the Amazon capital Themiscryra on the river Thermodon.
There he was to secure for Eurytheus' daughter the golden girdle
given by Ares to the Amazon queen. Accounts of what resulted vary
(with another hero, Theseus, taking a greater part as he superseded
Heracles in Attic cult) but the burden of the tale has Heracles
eventually take the trophy by force, sometimes killing or kidnapping
the queen or her sister, and returning with it to Greece.

Like Achilles, Heracles is associated with a complex sex antagonism (initiated by Hera literally in the womb when, hearing Zeus
announce that on that day a child of his would be born who would
rule the land, she arranged for the earlier birth of another of his
descendants) and legendary martial success. (13) But typologically
he is far closer to Bellerophon - like him obliged to perform a
series of heroic tasks to expiate crimes (Bellerophon's murder of
Bellerus and his own brother Deliades; Heracles' insane killing of
his children, two nephews - and in some versions - his first wife
Megara). It may be these similarities that permit him to supplant
Bellerophon, while the Achilles-Penthesilea story maintains a later-
al popularity.

Where literary sources are missing we have the evidence of Greek
ceramics. The first recognisable Amazons, on a terra-cotta votive
shield found at Tiryns, probably date from the eighth century. But
it is in the second quarter of the sixth century (575-550 BC) that
the subject becomes popular with vase-painters, 'arriving suddenly,
and in force, without any apparent antecedents'. (14) Almost all of
it is Attic - produced, that is, in Athens or that city's surrounds.

From the beginning the dominant theme is the battle between the
Greek heroes and the warrior women (known as 'Amazonomachies' from
the Greek root 'machy' - 'struggle'). The subject had obvious
compositional advantages for the silhouette style of black-figure
painting, but the abundance of martial episodes in Greek myth
negates this as the explanation of its popularity. ('The fight is
second in popularity only to the Lion and better represented than
most Labours in the second quarter of the century.' (15)) Nor does
it explain the frequency with which Heracles figures as the Amazons'
named or iconographically identifiable opponent.

We do know that Heracles is a central icon of the period, ac-
counting for some 44 per cent of all mythic representations on
Athenian vases. He often appears in conjunction with his patron,
the city's eponymous deity, Athena (an association which goes back
to even non-Athenian art in the seventh century). Belief in such
patronage not only canonised mythic figures, it was also used to
legitimate the claims of aspiring rulers.

Ehrenberg reminds us how important the local heroes were in a
region of culturally homogenous but competitive city-states:

The heroes had their special importance ... they were by their
graves and by their character of their cult more closely bound
to the soil than most of the gods; they represented a strong
element of intense religious life, and their cult formed the
centre of many small associations ... (which) could also grow
into a kind of representative of the state. The majority of the
heroes had once been great men of the epic stories and thus were
intimately associated with the form of life which belonged to the
times of the clans and their contests. They did their part in
breaking Greece up into its many political units; in the mythical contests between heroes the actual fights between states
found both model and expression. (16)

Interestingly, Heracles' Panhellenic importance exempts him from
Ehrenberg's observations (although it may make his cult that much
more appealing to an aspiring imperial power). And indeed he may
have been introduced into Athenian veneration through his mythic
connections with the city's goddess rather than any local association of his own. But however his cult was established, it was
sufficiently representative of the Athenian state to interest the
sixth-century politician Pisistratus.

In staging his repeated coups, this tyrant was rather given to
the 'beau geste'. (When we consider how important popular support
was to the tyrant's challenge to the aristocratic oligarchy, this
is not surprising.) Pisistratus' first seizure of power involved
his capture of the Acropolis, the city's citadel and its sacred
precinct. In attendance was a bodyguard armed with clubs, the
traditional weapon of Heracles in contemporary painting. A deliber-
ate reminiscence of the hero's much-represented Introduction to
Olympus? 'Promoting himself', Boardman argues, 'to be a neighbour
of the gods, of Athena in particular, might well appear a form of
apotheosis to the myth-minded.' (17)

After a brief reign, the tyrant was exiled. But his return to
Athens in the 550s was, if Herodotus is to be believed, even
flashier. This time the allusion to Athena's presentation of her
ward to the Olympians took the form of a charade: the politician
arranged for an unusually tall and comely woman to dress in full
armour and mount a chariot.

Then having rehearsed her in the most impressive pose to adopt,
they drove to the city where heralds who had been sent ahead
announced, according to their instructions, 'O Athenians, receive
Peistratos with friendly spirit. For Athena has favoured him
above all men and herself leads him to her acropolis.' (18)

Herodotus' account indicates Heracles' civic importance and the
way a politician might invoke his prestige. Since Pisistratus also
extensively patronised the arts, the abundance of visual motifs

representing 'his' hero's exploits, and perhaps even associating
them with his own achievements, is a logical development of the
period. (19)

But Heracles' dominance in this black-figure ware suggests a sub-
ordinate role for the Amazons. Admittedly the subject must have
held its own fascinations for artists, and the women are often
represented alone - but the coincidence of their popularity with the
Heraclean cult cannot be ignored. Without concluding that the production of the image is entirely dependent on interest in their
mythic male adversaries, we must note that the first important era
of Amazonian art occurred in a state which extensively venerated and
depicted their conqueror.

Pisistratus' administration of Athens was, despite its absolut-
ism, relatively humane and efficient and he was finally able to establish a degree of dynastic control. His sons ruled the city from
his death in 528 BC until 510, when the Spartans invaded to restore
oligarchy. The Pisistratids' deposition, like their rise, seems to
have coincided with changes in Attic iconography. In the first
quarter of the fifth century the predominance of the Heracles image
lessens significantly in black-figure ware and that of a parallel
hero, Theseus, increases (19.4 per cent and 13.2 per cent of total
mythic scenes respectively vs. 44 per cent and 5 per cent prior to
510). (20) (The final Heraclean Amazonomachy in Attic art occurs on
a 'metope' (a stone block with relief sculptures) in the mid-fifth
century Hephaisteion.) Perhaps Heracles was tainted with the unpop-
ularity of the deposed tyrant. More likely the newly established
Athenian democracy (c. 507 BC) and the rising threat of Persian invasion encouraged the development of a more peculiarly Athenian
cult. And certainly Heracles had a rustic impetuosity less and less
suitable to a population rapidly becoming urbanised. As Isocrates
(436-338 BC) notes in his 'Helen' (X, 24): 'It came to pass that
Heracles undertook perilous labours more celebrated and more severe,
Theseus those more useful, and to the Greeks of more vital importance.'

Did the Athenians find it necessary to replace him with a 'negative idealisation', in Philip Slater's terms, 'a kind of pastel
Heracles'? (21) The stylistic changes of the period, including the
opportunities for detail offered by the development of the red-
figure technique and the general adoption of classical illusionism,
could be argued to encourage a change to prettified and less totemic
heroes. (22)

THE THESEUS VARIANT

It may simply be our clearer vision of the later era, but Theseus
seems a remarkably synthetic figure, plucked from relative mythic
obscurity and fixed up with a retrospective genealogy in the traditional way. Nilsson suggests his importance to the fictive continuity of the Athenian state:
    the aspirations of which were, as usually happened, projected
    back into the mythical age ... during its heyday in the fifth
    century BC, he is made the hero of the Athenian democracy, the
    founder of the Athenian state through the synoecism (the unity

of the Attic peoples) and of the democratic institutions of
Athens. (23)

About 520 BC a poem was written (perhaps by the constitutionalist
Cleisthenes) attributing specifically Heraclean feats to the new
hero, making him a companion of the older figure in the Trojan war,
confronting him with giants on his journey from Troezen to Athens,
etc. Among these was his accompaniment of Heracles on the expedition against the Amazons.

Accounts of this episode again vary, moving from Theseus' lieu-
tenancy on the voyage (Heracles sometimes awards him a captured
Amazon bride in thanks for his aid) to command of one of his own.
The wedding of the two traditions is graphically evident in the
metopes of the Athenian treasury at Delphi, built sometime after the
establishment of post-Pisistratid democracy (c. 505 BC). (24) The
subjects of the metopes are threefold, and evidently interconnected:
the labours of Heracles, the labours of Theseus, and the battles of
the Greeks and the Amazons. The Amazonomachy is the unifying
device. Its position on the eastern face of the Treasury links the
easternmost metopes of the north and south - each showing an Amazon,
the former with Heracles, the latter with Theseus. The theme may
well be their joint expedition to Themiscyra.

Neither this iconography nor the Treasury itself can be precisely
related to Athenian politics, especially if it is too early to have
been built in commemoration of the Greek victory against the
Persians at Marathon in 490. But the newly propagandist direction
of these sculptures is significant, notably in one of the few non-
combatative metopes: 'Theseus and his patron Athene standing
quietly, as if in conversation.' (25) Another hero is promoted to
the Athenian pantheon, and the warrior women are conquered anew.
The patriotic theme circumscribes - and reconstructs - the myth.

The salient difference in the two heroes' campaigns against the
warrior women is that where Heracles returned with the queen's
stolen girdle, Theseus returns with the queen herself - a crucial
link to the new myth's centrepiece, the Amazons' retaliatory attack
on Athens. The original amatory adventure yields to an emphasis on
patriotic endeavour and local defence. (26)

By at least as early as the fifth century, the Theseia - the
Athenian festival honouring the hero's rescue of the citizens marked
for sacrifice to the Minotaur - was coupled with a memorial recalling his defeat of the Amazons. And soon the logistics of the
tribeswomen's attack on the city were written into the historical
record. Plutarch (b. before AD 50 - died after AD 120), citing the
fourth-century historian Cleidemus, reports that

the Amazons' left wing extended to what is now called the
Amazoneum, while their right rested on the Pnyx, at the point
where the gilded figure of Victory now stands ... the Athenians
engaged the left wing, attacking it from the Museum, and ... the
tombs of those who fell are on either side of the street leading
to the gate near the shrine of the hero Chalcodon, which is now
known as the Piraeic gate. On this flank, he (Cleidemus) tells
us, the women routed the Athenians and forced them back as far as
the shrine of the Eumenides. But on the other side, the
Athenians who attacked the Amazons from the Palladium and
Ardettus and the Lyceum, drove their right wing back to the

camp and killed great numbers of them. Cleidemus adds that after
three months a peace was arranged through Hippolyta. (27)

How did this tradition of Amazon attack arise? The Athenians
may, for various political and demographic reasons, have enjoyed
something of a siege mentality. They also had a propensity to
mythologise unascribable graves or monuments. But if any historical
event encouraged their elaboration of mythology, it was the Persian
Wars. From the mid-sixth century the Greek colonies in western Asia
(Ionia) were threatened by the rising strength of the Persians, who
took over and enlarged the empire of the Medes from 550 BC. In 499
BC Athens and Eretria aided an unsuccessful Ionian rebellion. Nine
years later the Persians sent a punitive invasion across the Aegean.
Eretria was sacked, but the Athenians were victorious at Marathon.
(And a rumour spread of Theseus' ghostly deliverance of his country-
men: 'Many of the men who fought the Medes at Marathon', writes
Plutarch, 'believed that they saw the apparition of Theseus, clad in
full armour and charging ahead of them against the barbarians.'
(28)) A decade later, in 480, Xerxes mounted a larger invasion,
reaching Athens and securing the entire eastern part of continental
Greece. Attica was evacuated and its capital sacked by the invaders. Yet somehow in the following year the weak and divided
Greek states managed to rout the invaders decisively.

Athens, with Plataea and Megara the only states to refuse submission from the outset, saw the victory in literally epic terms.
The defeated power joined the catalogue of heroic enemies overcome
by the state, and Robert Drews notes that 'Later orators who spoke
in praise of Athens included as a standard "topos" the recital of
Athens' defense of Greece against the Amazons, Eumolpus' Thracians
and Xerxes' Persians.' (29) Thus Isocrates' (436-338 BC)
'Panegyricus', cited at the beginning of this essay.

As the historic attack by one group of Asiatics was assimilated
into the record, it had a reciprocal effect on the myths about
another. One explanation is that both parties came to be identifiedd
with a barbarism deservedly crushed by civilisation, but this is
probably an overstatement. Certainly the Persians were not treated
contemptuously in the resulting commemorations. Their triumphs over
the era's major civilisations were soberly respected. 'It was precisely because the Greeks appreciated the significance of the fall
of Lydia, Babylon and Egypt that their own victory over the Persians
stood out as an event not paralleled since the Trojan Wars.' (30)

If anything, both Xerxes' invaders and their mythic Asian
counterparts may have consolidated each other's place in the enemy
pantheon. From the second quarter of the sixth century (i.e. long
before the invasion) Amazons in black-figure painting are sometimes
kitted out in fanciful elements of 'oriental' costume: wicker
shields, phrygian caps, geometric motley. With the development in
detail offered by the red-figure technique, this practice was intensified, and then transferred back to the Persians. The first
half of the fifth century sees Xerxes' warriors in costumes by that
time associated with the Amazons!

This new heroic configuration was again invoked by Athenian politicians. A decade after the Persians' defeat, Cimon, a general in
the Athenian-led Delian League, bid for the leadership of what was
by then an imperial power. His rival, Themistocles, derived his

prestige from his participation in the naval victory against the
Persians at Salamis. Cimon (who had also distinguished himself in
this battle) could counter with his father Miltiades' generalship at
Marathon, a heritage which he sought to make good by an even more
explicit identification with that battle's patron, Theseus. Recalling an oracular injunction to return the hero's remains to the
city, he sought out the island of Skyros while on a naval patrol.
The traditional burial place, Plutarch tells us, providentially
yielded up some unusually imposing remains - a very large skeleton
interred with a bronze spear and sword.

> He had the bones placed on board his trireme and brought them
> back with great pomp and ceremony to the hero's native land,
> almost four hundred years after he had left it. This affair did
> more than any other achievement of Cimon's to endear him to the
> people. (31)

The result was the eclipse and eventual ostracism of Themistocles, the rise of his rival and the consolidation of Theseus' place
in the city's devotions. The return of the hero to his city was
annually celebrated in a state festival (the Theseia referred to
previously) and a memorial erected to house his bones. Again political purposes were to shape Amazon iconography.

The commemorative Theseion was a large public assembly place,
serving as a council chamber, armoury, and refuge for slaves and
the poor. The decorations included a trio of wall-paintings by
Micon, a painter and sculptor associated with the pro-Cimon party.
These no longer survive, but Aristophanes alludes in the
'Lysistrata' to Micon's painting of mounted Amazons, and the
second-century-AD guidebook of the Greek geographer Pausanias
describes the scenes on each wall: Athenians fighting Amazons,
Theseus battling with the Centaurs, and his recovery of a ring which
King Minos, challenging his descent from Poseidon, had thrown into
the sea.

A decade after Themistocles' exile, Cimon too grew unpopular and
was finally forced to leave the city. But an upswing in his political fortunes returned him to power and stimulated a spate of even
more explicitly political mythmaking, once again featuring the
Amazons. At this time (c. 460 BC) Cimon's brother-in-law Peisianax
erected the 'Stoa Poikile' or Painted Portico in Athens. (32) It
was decorated by a contemporary of Micon's, the muralist Polygnotus
of Thasos. The painter's associations with Cimon were considerable
- enough for him to be the rumoured lover of his sister Elpinice
(whose features supposedly found their way into one of the Portico's
paintings), although Plutarch argues that there was no personal com-
mission; Polygnotus 'undertook the work for nothing, simply out of
the desire to honour his city'. (33) In any event, the civic-
spirited painter honoured Athens' leading citizen: the murals,
Pausanias reports, juxtaposed 1. combat between the Athenians and
the Spartans; 2. the Greeks after the capture of Troy; 3. Theseus
leading the Athenians against the Amazons; and 4. the Battle of
Marathon, featuring Theseus and a prominently displayed figure of
Cimon's father, Miltiades.

These monumental Amazonomachies both reaffirmed and modified the
traditional images. The theme of conflict with the State and its
founding fathers was evidently maintained, but stylistic and technical developments wrought significant changes.

Polygnotan classicism - developing perspective, a denser and more
'realistic' composition - is thought to have directly influenced the
art of ceramic painting. So, perhaps, did Polygnotan iconography.
As Giovanni Becatti argues:

In the fervid pictorial climate of the Athens of Cimon, it is no
wonder that Attic vase painters, working to renew their own
language, should have drawn inspiration from the rich figurative
world of the Polygnotan school. It therefore seems legitimate to
look for ideas and motifs from Polygnotos' and Mikon's painting
in the enormous corpus of vases. A whole group of red-figure
vases which develop the theme of the Amazonomachy show compo-
sitions of Amazons on horseback, or on their knees, or retreat-
ing. The fact that these motifs constantly recur in similar
forms bears witness to their derivation from a common archetype,
diversely transmitted and reformulated; this archetype could
indeed have been the painting of Mikon. (34)

The red-figure technique, as noted previously, permitted a richer
detail than its black-figure predecessor, a richness sometimes
heightened in the mid-fifth century by the use of added colour. The
Amazonomachies on the vases of the period may result from the con-
vergence of such technical opportunity, the stylistic influences of
the monumental muralists, and the political and artistic suitability
of these combat scenes. Thus, commentators argue, the rocky terrain
where the Amazon battled on the Areopagus could now be effectively
rendered by a change from a single baseline to an uneven ground.

This tendency to elaboration had other effects on the motif: it
permitted the painter further to characterise his subjects as
foreign, female, and - though here commentaries have over-sentiment-
alised - erotically conquered.

Perhaps the fullest treatment in this vein is the 'Penthesilea'
cup-tondo by the artist known today as the Berlin painter. The ex-
pressiveness of this painting has prompted a great deal of comment,
much of it highly speculative - notably the ascription of its
subject to Achilles' fatal wounding of the Amazon queen. If, as
von Bothmer argues, its unusual size and colour are owed to the
Polygnotan murals, might it not also derive its subject there? (In
which case the cup depicts the Amazons against the Athenians, not
the Trojan wars.) (35) And if the cup is, in some sense, related to
a project celebrating the Athenian state, what does that suggest
about the phallocratic possibilities in the patriotic theme?

Compared with the severe silhouettes of the black-figure period
the Penthesilea scene seems like a close-up, its depiction both
emotionalised and, despite the gravity of its subject, somehow
'decorated'. The protagonists' costumes, for instance, have been
richly, and most fictively, exoticised. Robertson notes that the
painter has combined Greek and 'alien' fashions to achieve the
colourful Amazon ensembles and 'is not concerned with actual
practice either in his own day or in the supposed time of the heroic
scene. To enrich his design he rings the changes in Greek and
foreign costume.' (36)

Then there is, given the painting's vivid physicality, the
subject of the main protagonists' confrontation. Is this the
poignant exchange of a victorious Achilles ruefully contemplating
his reproachful foe, or simply an evocative movement of conscious

victory and conscious defeat? However we interpret it, there is no
ignoring the deliberation with which the painter focuses on the subordination of the Amazon, not just as foe, but as woman. If
previous Amazonomachies brought patriotic concerns to an image of
sexual conflict (and in doing so provided the impetus for that
image's dissemination), the Penthesilea cup returns the sexual to
the military episode with a vengeance.

4   THE PARTHENON AMAZONOMACHIES

The apotheosis of the patriotic Amazonomachy occurs in the Parthenon
- itself the apotheosis of Athenian state art. In size, in situation and in subject, the temple of the city's presiding deity was
designed to proclaim Athenian power.
    Begun in 447 BC, at the instigation of Cimon's successor Peri-
cles, the Parthenon was part of a massive building (and public
employment) programme financed largely by tribute from the Athenian-
led Delian League. The cult to which it was dedicated, that of
Athena 'Parthenos', or virgin, can itself be interpreted as a
strident expression of patriarchal ideology. Not only is Athena the
inveterate ally of Greek heroes against her Olympian sisters, not
only does she abjure the 'feminine' functions of coupling and
childbirth, not only is her physical sexuality swathed in male
armour - but her mythic parentage (portrayed on the temple's east
pediment) presents her as born only of the Father:
    Zeus married Metis (Wisdom), got her with child, and then
    swallowed her, fearing a prophecy that she would later bear
    another child who should be stronger than he. After a period of
    gestation, seized with a fearful pain in the head, he called on
    Hephaestus (or in some versions Prometheus) to split it open with
    axe or hammer; which performed, out sprang Athene armed 'cap a
    pie'. (37)
The temple of this patroness was decorated with images so explicitly and unusually secular in their concerns as to provoke
charges of impiety. Around the wall of the interior building, or
'cella', ran a frieze portraying the annual Panathenaic procession
of the citizens honouring their goddess, 'the first and one of the
very few surviving cases where a mortal activity is represented on
a Greek temple instead of something from divine or heroic mythology'. (38)
    The outside of this temple was decorated with metopes depicting
combat with the traditional enemies - 1. the Greeks against the
Centaurs, 2. the Gods against the Giants, 3. the sack of Troy, and
4. the Greeks against the Amazons - opponents which at least one
commentator has described as 'variously superhuman, inhuman,
subhuman, or non-human ... a general background of conflict for
the human state'. (39)
    Two of these images - the Gigantomachy and the Amazonomachy -
were also inscribed on the shield of the temple's cult statue, a
huge ivory and gold colossus of the armed deity brandishing an image
of Victory. The sculptor was Phidias, the director of the entire
project and a friend and supporter of Pericles. Phidias' Amazono-

machy, like the Polygnotan murals, is thought to have explicitly
identified the Athenian leadership with the victorious Greeks.
Plutarch writes that

> in the relief of the battle of the Amazons, which is represented
> on the shield of the goddess, he carved a figure representing
> himself as a bald old man lifting up a stone with both hands, and
> also ... he introduced a particularly fine likeness of Pericles
> fighting an Amazon. The position of the hand, which holds a
> spear in front of Pericles' face, seems to have been ingeniously
> contrived to conceal the resemblance, but it can still be seen
> quite plainly from either side. (40)

Neither the Parthenon colossus nor its accoutrements survive, and
extant copies do not correspond precisely to Plutarch's description.
Among these, however, the Lenormant copy does bear a figure hurling
a rock with both hands, while the Strangford shield includes a
warrior with a spear. The latter figure's dominant place in the
composition has also prompted an identification with Theseus. 'Is
it he, or is it Pericles? Or is it both, Theseus appearing as, and
identified with, Pericles.' (41) The evidence is inconclusive, but
perhaps it can be little else. As the city's 'past' was constructed
in opposition to such as the mythic heroines, its historical personages became ineluctably mythologised.

The Parthenon Amazonomachies may seem, in their conscious contra-
position of the forces of the State and its female enemies, to be
the climax of the genre. They are anyway among the final works of
their kind. The fourth century saw the decline of Athens from imperial pre-eminence and its artistic celebration. But the traditional encounter between Greek patriarch and female warrior did
not yet pass out of currency. It would find its way into the
exploits of still another mythologised leader, the Macedonian
conqueror, Alexander the Great.

5   THE ATHENIAN PATRIARCHY

We have seen how the myth of Athens' triumph over the Amazons was
used to historicise the claims of that state. In his 'Funeral
Oration' the Athenian orator Lysias (c. 459-380 BC) joins that
patriotic theme to another:

> They (the Amazons) would not return home and report their own
> misfortune and our ancestors' valour; for they perished on the
> spot, and were punished for their folly, making our city's memory
> imperishable in its valour; while owing to their disaster in
> this region, they rendered their own country nameless. And so
> these women, by their unjust greed for others' land, justly lost
> their own.

As victory thrust the Athenian state into immortality, so defeat
removed the Amazons from history altogether, effectively expunging
them from the record.

In the light of the former's concern to construct just such a
record, the condemnation of the warrior women to literal, and literary, extinction seems pointed. And the provocative phrase 'they
rendered their own country nameless' suggests an expulsion from a

Symbolic Order (the named, or spoken, past) consonant with the
Lacanian view of the patriarchal control of (history as) language.
But the burden of Lysias' argument, and the one I wish to pursue,
is that these women deserved it.

In her survey of the myths of female rule, Joan Bamberger
challenges Bachofen's famous reading of the Amazon story as 'real
and not poetic'. As she argues,

> Myth may become through repeated recitation a moral history of
> action while not in itself a detailed chronology of recorded
> events. Myth may be part of culture history in providing justi-
> fication for a present and perhaps permanent reality by giving an
> invented 'historical' explanation of how this reality was
> created. (42)

Bamberger's study of a group of South American myths leads her to
observe

> the ideological thrust of the argument made in the myth of the
> Rule of Women, and the justification it offers for male dominance
> through the evocation of a vision of a catastrophic alternative -
> a society dominated by women. The myth, in its reiteration that
> women did not know how to handle power when in possession of it,
> reaffirms dogmatically the inferiority of their present position.
> (43)

The Amazon tradition offered the Athenians precisely such a
justification, and they needed it. For economic, political and
demographic reasons, the women of that state suffered an institutionalised subordination radical even by the standards of their
Greek predecessors and contemporaries.

Perhaps the best expression of their plight remains Lewis H.
Morgan's writing in his 'Ancient Society':

> It still remains an enigma that a race, with endowments great
> enough to impress their mental life upon the world, should have
> remained essentially barbarian in their treatment of the female
> sex at the height of their civilization. Women were not treated
> with cruelty, nor with discourtesy within the range of the privi-
> leges allowed them; but their education was superficial, inter-
> course with the opposite sex was denied them, and their inferi-
> ority was inculcated as a principle, until it came to be accepted
> as a fact by the women themselves. (44)

But Morgan overemphasises the enigmatic character of this oppression, contradictory as it may seem in such an enlightened
culture. In the same work he speculates on the influence which the
accumulation of private property may have had on the gentile
(tribal) organisation of archaic Athens:

> The growth of the idea of property, and the rise of monogamy,
> furnished motives sufficiently powerful to demand and obtain this
> change (from the female line to the male) in order to bring
> children into the gens of their father, and into a participation
> in the inheritance of his estate.... The pertinacity with which
> the principle was maintained down to the time of Solon, that
> property should remain in the gens of the deceased owner, illus-
> trates the vitality of the organization through all these
> periods. It was this rule which compelled the heiress to marry
> in her own gens to prevent a transfer of the property by her
> marriage to another gens. When Solon allowed the owner of

property to dispose of it by will, in case he had no children, he made the first inroad upon the property rights of the gens. (45)

Solon's sixth-century reforms reorganised Athenian society to meet the demands of a new economy founded on maritime and monetary supremacy and the labours of an increasingly large slave class. This legislation included the licensing of state brothels staffed by slaves, the abolition of the sale of children into slavery - excepting that of an unmarried non-virgin woman by her male guardian, and severe penalties for adultery. It was aimed, argues historian Sarah Pomeroy, 'at eliminating strife among men and strengthening the newly created democracy. Women are a perennial source of friction among men. Solon's solution to this problem was to keep them out of sight and to limit their influence.' (46)

The effect of this legislation persisted, even intensified, in the next century. As Athens grew into an imperial power, its population (the largest of the Greek states) was further stratified into a dominant layer of some 300 wealthy families; a nominal citizenry of 30,000-40,000 (the majority of these, the much poorer 'hoplite' and 'thete' classes, comprising urban craftsmen, poor peasants and the like); a large number of 'metics' or non-citizen foreigners, who were forbidden landownership but permitted to engage in the city's trading and industrial enterprises, and some 80,000-100,000 slaves, performing fieldwork, domestic service, and artisanal functions. (47)

The chief obligation of citizen women in these circumstances was the production of male heirs to meet the demands of war and familial continuity (the citizenry was seen to be composed of the 'oikoi', its family units) without exceeding the already overstretched resources of an enlarging leisure class. Heiresses of families without sons were deemed 'attached to the family property', which went with her to her husband, and thence to their child. Widowed heiresses were obliged to marry their nearest male kinsman.

Conjugal sexual abstinence, female infanticide, male homosexuality (but not female, neither opportunity nor ideology supported such a practice), and rigorous penalties for adultery were established features of such a situation. So was a dowry to ensure a daughter's marriageability, and responsible fathers did not raise more daughters than they could adequately provide for. Marriages were arranged by fathers for political and economic considerations, the optimum age being considered 14 for the bride and 30 for the groom. The bride could then look forward to passing from the guardianship of her father to that of her husband (legally, women never came of age) and a short, arduous and secluded life.

In the home women's work was often performed - and associated with - that of slaves. To a leisured male ruling class which condemned most manual labour as 'banausic' (unfit for citizens) this lowered female status went even further, condemning even the spinning and household administration of upper-class women to servility.

The resulting tension between the Athenian State and its female members found its way into artistic expression:

Many tragedies show women in rebellion against the established norms of society. As the 'Oresteia' of Aeschylus makes clear, a city-state such as Athens flourished only through the breaking

of familial or blood bonds and the subordination of the patriarchal family within the patriarchal state. But women were in
conflict with this political principle, for their interests were
private and family-related. Thus, drama often shows them acting
out of the women's quarters, and concerned with children,
husbands, fathers, brothers, and religions deemed more primitive
and family-oriented than the Olympian, which was the support of
the state. (48)

Read in such a context, the Amazon myths can be interpreted as an
expression of this unease. Their threat, like that of the adulterous Phaedra, or the homicidal Deianara, was a reversal of the ex-
tremity of their oppression: 'that some day the vanquished would
arise and treat their ex-masters as they themselves had been
treated.' (49)

The Amazon myth resolved this tension by representing such a
rebellion as already concluded in deserved defeat. Lysias suggests
that greed for land was the source of the tribeswomen's downfall.
The association of their image with primitive, chaotic or alien
forces (the Centaurs, the Giants, the Trojans and the Persians)
produces similar justifications. So, interestingly, do the folk
etymologies invented by the Greeks in explanation of a name whose
derivation was already lost.

Perhaps the most famous of these is 'a-mastos', variously trans-
latable as 'breastless', 'not brought up by the breast', 'beings
with strong breasts', and 'with one breast'. This has been suggested as the source of the tradition that the Amazons excised one
breast to further their military prowess (a tradition notably absent
from both Greek art and myth; although the physician Hippocrates
does say that the women of the Sauromatae, identified by his older
contemporary Herodotus as the descendants of Amazons and Scythian
men, seared the right breast of their female infants to divert
strength to the right arm and shoulder). (50)

Other retrospective etymologies include 'a-maza', 'without barley
bread'; 'azona', 'chastity belt'; and 'amazosas', 'opposed to
man'. What is significant in these inventions is their characterisation of the warrior women as anti-feminine, self-mutilating, man-
hating and technically underdeveloped. (The suggestion that they
could not grow barley is not atypical: another account suggests
that they had to detour hundreds of miles overland on their expedition from Asia Minor to Athens because they had no knowledge of
sailing, and usually the women are presented as virtually without
culture.)

Where the Greeks could not christen their enemies, they invented
etymologies; where they could - in the individual Amazon names inscribed on vases or in the myths - the choices are again significant. Several of these names link the women with their traditional
animal, the horse: 'Hippolyte', 'of the stampeding horse';
'Melanippe', 'black mare'; 'Alcippe', 'powerful mare', etc.
Others convey a homicidal threat: 'Molpadia', 'death song';
'Penthesilea', 'compelling men to mourn'. (51) Did such bestial,
murderous beings deserve better than annihilation at the hands of
civilisation?

THE INIMITABLE HEROINE

A peculiar thing has happened in the case of the account we have
of the Amazons; for our accounts of other peoples keep a distinction between the mythical and the historical elements; for
the things that are ancient and false and monstrous are called
myths, but history wishes for the truth, whether ancient or
recent, and contains no monstrous element, or else only rarely.
But as regards the Amazons, the same stories are told now as in
early times, though they are marvellous and beyond belief. For
instance, who could believe that any army of women, or a city,
or a tribe, could ever be organised without men, and not only be
organised, but even make inroads upon the territory of other
people, and not only over power the peoples near them to the
extent of advancing as far as what is now Ionia, but even send
an expedition across the sea as far as Attica? For this is the
same as saying that the men of those times were women and that
the women were men (Strabo, 'Geography', 11.5.3).
The dilemma of the Greek writer Strabo (c. 64 BC - AD 21) still
perplexes us. In part, it can be resolved by the reading of
Athenian history suggested here - a reading which leads us to conclude that its object was not 'truth', but the construction of a
periodicised basis for the hegemony of the patriarchal state. But
if we could somehow ignore this 'history', and its inbuilt lesson of
female inferiority, what of the Amazon triumphant? Is the idea of
'autonomous warrior women' invariably paradoxical in patriarchal
culture? Can it resolve itself only in the reversal of the sexes,
making the heroines into their opponents, men?
As victor or vanquished, feminists have argued, the Amazons are
structured within the same terms of dominance and militarism:
If a matriarchy did develop ... it would necessarily have been a
society based on the exchange of men and probably on their
exploitation and oppression as well. Consequently the Amazons,
as an antidote for female subservience, are not as attractive as
some feminists have assumed. (52)
In 'The Guerrilleres' (a contemporary reworking of the Amazon
theme) Wittig retains the martial ideals as epic, wrongly, I
think: no struggle is as glorious or as triumphant as that. To
suggest it is to accept male values. (53)
Nor was Strabo alone among the ancients in relegating the
achievements of the Amazons to the sphere of the marvellous, the
supranatural. (54) In his fourth-century-AD 'Posthomerica', the
Byzantine poet Quintus Smyrnaeus describes a debate among the Trojan
women as they watch the exploits of Penthesilea from their city's
walls:

                              Suddenly
A fiery passion for the fray hath seized
Antimachus' daughter, Meneptolemus' wife
Tisiphone. Her heart waxed strong, and filled
With lust of fight she cried to fellows all,
With desperate-daring words, to spur them on
To woeful war, by recklessness made strong:
'Friends, let a heart of valour in our breasts
Awake!' Let us be like our lords, who fight

With foes for fatherland, for babes, for us.
And never pause for breath in that stern strife!
Let us too throne war's spirit in our hearts!
Let us too face the fight which favoureth none!
For we, we women, be not creatures cast
In diverse mould from men: to us is given
Such energy of life as stirs in them.
Eyes have we like to theirs, and limbs: throughout
Fashioned we are alike; one common light
We look on, and one common air we breathe:
With like food are we nourished: - nay, wherein
Have we been dowered of God more niggardly
Than men? Then let us shrink not from the fray!
See ye not yonder a woman far excelling
Men in the grapple of fight?

But the poet, aware as Tisiphone is not of the doom impending
upon both the Trojan men and their Amazon allies, posits a prudent
intervention by 'one voice of wisdom', the dissuasive Theano:

                                    for your strength
Can never be as that of Danaan men,
Men trained on daily battle. Amazons
Have joyed in ruthless fight, in charging steeds
From the beginning: all the toil of men
Do they endure, and therefore evermore
The spirit of the War-god thrills them through,
They fall not short of men in anything;
Their labour-hardened frames make great their hearts
For all achievement; never faint their knees
Nor tremble. Rumour speaks their queen to be
A daughter of the mighty Lord of War.
Therefore no woman may compare with her
In prowess - if she be a woman, not
A God come down in answer to our prayers.
    Yea, if our blood be all the race of men,
Yet unto diverse labours still they turn.
And that for each is evermore the best
Whereto he bringeth skill of use and wont.
Therefore do ye from tumult of the fray
Hold you aloof, and in your women's bowers
Before the loom still pace ye to and fro;
And war shall be the business of our lords.

Here the exploits of the Amazons only serve to confirm sexual
dimorphism and the sexual division of labour. Their successes
literally remove them from female comparison, rendering them either
masculine or divine. Nothing of the real oppression of their sex is
challenged by these mythic heroines, it is merely transcended. As
the lecture sequence of Mulvey and Wollen's film 'Penthesilea' observes: 'their weapons and strategy are men's weapons and strategy.
They offer a solution which is magical not political.' (55)

This said, is it none the less possible to extract a kernel of
female potency from the patriarchal shell? Can the Amazon myths,
like Engels's postulation of a communistic past in which 'the position of women is not only free, but honourable', function as an
historical white lie, freeing our aspirations from a legacy of un-

varied defeat? Can we break with history, remaking its images as we chose?

In her preface to 'The Lesbian Body', the novelist Monique Wittig compares two autonomies, that of the contemporary Women's Movement and its mythical precursors:

We already have our islets, our islands, we are already in process of living in a culture that befits us. The Amazons are women who live among themselves, by themselves and for themselves at the generally accepted levels: fictional, symbolic, actual. Because we are illusionary for traditional male culture we make no distinction between the three levels. Our reality is the fictional as it is socially accepted, our symbols deny the traditional symbols and are fictional for traditional male culture, and we possess an entire fiction into which we project ourselves and which is already a possible reality. It is our fiction that validates us. (56)

Without denying the force of ideology, one might reply that it is not the fiction of female resistance which validates our struggles, but its reality.

As this essay has attempted to show, the construction of the Amazon myth cannot be separated from a context of patriarchal dominance. But the context has developed to generate women's resistance. Much as it inspired feminist struggle, was not Victorian matriarchalism also its product, an acknowledgment of the female power already manifest in the new economic formation? The same, I think, can be said of present searches for a militant female past. The findings may, as in the case of the Amazons, be ultimately inappropriable. But the project itself encourages. Would it have commenced without our genuine identification with women in struggle - a new will to power born of the unease of our own patriarchal era?

NOTES

1 Unless otherwise indicated, this and all other classical quotations are from the Loeb Classical Library editions of the named author, edited by T.E.Page, E.Capps, and W.H.D.Rouse, London, Heinemann.
2 Adrienne Rich, The Kingdom of the Fathers, 'Partisan Review', vol. XLIII, no.1, 1976, p.25.
3 Elizabeth Gould Davis, 'The First Sex', London, Dent, 1973, p.339.
4 Johann Jacob Bachofen, 'Myth, Religion and Mother Right', trans. Ralph Manheim, London, Routledge & Kegan Paul, 1967, p.109.
5 Donald J.Sobol, 'The Amazons of Greek Mythology', London, Thomas Yoseloff, 1972, p.122.
6 Mina Zografou, 'Amazons in Homer and Hesiod', Athens, 1972, p.14.
7 Martin P.Nilsson, 'The Mycenaean Origin of Greek Mythology', Cambridge University Press, 1932, p.215.
8 Proclus' work is also known to us indirectly, through the 'Biblioteca' of Photius, a ninth-century-AD Byzantine scholar.
9 G.L.Huxley, 'Greek Epic Poetry from Eumelos to Panyassis', London, Faber & Faber, 1969, p.148.

10 As cited in Florence Mary Bennett, 'Religious Cults Associated
    with the Amazons', New York, Columbia University Press, 1912,
    p.3.
11 As cited in Zografou, op.cit., p.20.
12 Notably those of Pindar and Euripides (fifth century BC),
    Lycrophon (fourth century BC), Apollodorus (second century BC),
    Plutarch and Diodorus Siculus (first century AD) and Justin
    (third century AD).
13 For a detailed account of this, cf. Philip Slater, 'The Glory
    of Hera', Boston, Beacon Press, 1971, pp.337-96.
14 Dietrich von Bothmer, 'Amazons in Greek Art', London, Oxford
    University Press, 1957, p.6.
15 John Boardman, 'Athenian Black Figure Vases', London, Thames &
    Hudson, 1974, p.223.
16 Victor Ehrenberg, 'The Greek State', London, Methuen, 1969,
    p.17.
17 John Boardman, Herakles, Peisistratos and Sons, 'Revue Archae-
    ologique', vol. I, 1972, p.62.
18 Herodotus, I, 60, as cited in ibid.
19 Ibid., pp.65-6. Boardman also notes that Pisistratus named a
    son of his Thessalos, the name of one of Heracles' sons in the
    'Iliad'.
20 John Boardman, Herakles, Peisistratos and Eleusis, 'Journal of
    Hellenic Studies', vol. XCV, 1975, pp.1-2.
21 Slater, op.cit., p.389.
22 T.B.L.Webster, 'Everyday Life in Classical Athens', London,
    Batsford, 1965, p.102, also notes a humanising of the mythic
    enemies: 'It is characteristic of the new attitude of the late
    sixth century that (although the Krommyan sow and the bull of
    Marathon are included) they conceive of danger mostly in terms
    not of dangerous animals but of monstrous men.'
23 Nilsson, op.cit., p.163
24 The date of its building is often put after the Battle of
    Marathon (490 BC) because of a (probably erroneous) attribution
    of a dedicatory inscription by Pausanias. Both von Bothmer and
    C.M.Robertson argue that it probably antedates 490. Cf. von
    Bothmer, op.cit., p.118 and Charles Martin Robertson, 'A History
    of Greek Art', Cambridge University Press, 1975, pp.167-8.
25 Ibid., p.170.
26 W.R.Connor, Ruth B.Edwards, Simon Tidworthy, Anne G.Ward, 'The
    Quest for Theseus', London, Pall Mall Press, 1970, p.41.
27 Plutarch, 'The Rise and Fall of Athens', trans. Ian Scott-
    Kilvert, Harmondsworth, Penguin, 1960, p.33.
28 Ibid., pp.40-1.
29 Robert Drews, 'The Greek Accounts of Eastern History',
    Cambridge, Mass., Center for Hellenic Studies, 1973, p.35.
30 Ibid., p.67.
31 Plutarch, op.cit., p.150.
32 Von Bothmer, op.cit., p.200, notes a possible allusion to the
    Portico's original name, the Peisianakteion, in the Amazon name
    'Peisianassa' inscribed on a contemporary bell-krater. Similar-
    ly, the appearance of the unusual Amazon name 'Dolope' on
    another krater of the period may allude to the Dolopians, tra-
    ditionally held to have been expelled from Skyros by Cimon when
    he secured the bones of Theseus.

33 Plutarch, op.cit., p.145.
34 Giovanni Becatti, 'The Art of Ancient Greece and Rome', trans. John Ross, London, Thames & Hudson, 1968, p.148.
35 Von Bothmer, op.cit., pp.147-8.
36 Charles Martin Robertson, 'Greek Painting', Geneva, Skira, 1959, p.120.
37 Robertson, 'A History of Greek Art', p.301.
38 Ibid., p.296.
39 C.M.Bowra, 'Periclean Athens', London, Weidenfeld & Nicolson, 1971, p.112.
40 Plutarch, op.cit., p.198.
41 Connor, Edwards, Tidworthy, Ward, op.cit., p.170.
42 Joan Bamberger, The Myth of Matriarchy: Why Men Rule in Primitive Society, in 'Woman, Culture and Society', ed. Michelle Z. Rosaldo and Louise Lamphere, Stanford, California, Stanford University Press, 1974, p.267. (Bachofen's own theory of a matriarchal stage in human history can itself be read as a justification of eventual patriarchy, refurbished on social darwinist lines. Cf. Elizabeth Fee, The Sexual Politics of Victorian Social Anthropology, in 'Clio's Consciousness Raised', ed. Mary Hartman and Lois W.Banner, New York, Harper & Rowe, 1974, pp.90-2.)
43 Bamberger, op.cit., p.279.
44 Lewis H.Morgan, 'Ancient Society', Cambridge, Mass., Harvard University Press, 1964, p.401.
45 Ibid., p.201.
46 Sarah B.Pomeroy, 'Goddesses, Whores, Wives and Slaves', London, Robert Hale, 1976, p.57.
47 Perry Anderson, 'Passages from Antiquity to Feudalism', London, New Left Books, 1974, p.38.
48 Pomeroy, op.cit., p.97.
49 Ibid.
50 Sobol, op.cit., pp.111-12. The Latin historians Diodorus Siculus (2.45.3) and Justin (2.4.9-10) do record the tradition in later writings (first and third centuries AD, respectively).
51 Sobol, op.cit., p.162.
52 Mary Kelly, review of 'Penthesilea', 'Spare Rib', no.30, p.42.
53 Sophie Dick, review of 'The Lesbian Body', 'Spare Rib', no.41, p.45.
54 Similarly, Lysias writes of the Amazons: 'They were accounted as men for their high courage, rather than as women for their sex; so much more did they seem to excel men in their spirit than to be at a disadvantage in their form' ('Funeral Oration', 4-5).
55 As cited by Mary Kelly, op.cit. For other discussions of 'Penthesilea' cf. Claire Johnston and Paul Willeman, Penthesilea, Queen of the Amazons, 'Screen', vol.XV, no.3, 1974, and Laura Mulvey and Peter Wollen, Written Discussion, 'Afterimage', no.6, 1976, pp.30-9.
56 Monique Wittig, 'The Lesbian Body', London, Peter Owen, 1975, pp.9-10.

THE WOMAN-POWER

Joanna Southcott was a messianic prophetess whose teachings acquired
a very large following in early nineteenth-century England. From a
close examination of her heretical writings it can be seen that they
contained an implicit challenge to male authority and an assertion
to female spiritual power. With the development of the Owenite
socialist movement in the 1830s, her language of defiance became a
source of inspiration to a number of socialist feminists, particularly the leaders of the Communist Church.

Chapter 6

The Woman-Power

Religious heresy and feminism in
early English socialism

Barbara Taylor

ACKNOWLEDGMENTS

For useful comments and encouragement in writing this essay, my
thanks to Susan Lipshitz, Mandy Merck, Trevor Evans, Gareth Stedman
Jones's seminar group in Cambridge, and particularly to Eileen Yeo,
whose own work on radicalism and religion influenced me greatly and
without whose guidance and criticism the essay would not have been
written. My thanks also to the staff of the Reading Room at the
British Museum and the University of London Library at Senate House
for their assistance, and to the Canada Council of Arts and Science
for their financial support during my period of research.

In 1792, the year of the publication of Mary Wollstonecraft's
'Vindication of the Rights of Women', a middle-aged domestic servant
in Devon called Joanna Southcott began to hear Voices. After
several months in which they interrupted her housework with their
mysterious prophecies, the Voices told Joanna that she was the new
saviour, the 'Woman Clothed with the Sun' of the Biblical Reve-
lations, sent to deliver mankind from the Fall. 'These words were
so terrible', Joanna later wrote, 'they made me tremble.' In 1802,
after the publication of a little tract on the coming apocalypse,
(1) she was encouraged by her small band of followers - mostly
clerical gentlemen with a history of allegiance to chiliastic
prophets - to leave Devon for London. After eighteen months of
intense activity, carefully stage-managed by her backers, 8,000
persons had declared themselves converts. (2) By 1808 more than
14,000 had bought the sealed paper which was the token of the
Joannaite, and by the time of her death in 1814 the number may have
swelled to 100,000 in the London area alone, (3) with many thousands
more in the industrial north.
How many of these converts were women we do not know. But one
hostile observer referred to them as a 'petticoat republic' made up
of 'old women', and certainly many of Joanna's poetic prophecies
appear to have been directed at a female following:
Fear not ye women; fear not ... My Mother; fear not, My Sister

- I will be your Saviour - I will be your Conqueror - I will
tread the liar between My Feet; he shall feel the weight of my
fury; he shall tremble and fall before ME. (4)
'Is it a new thing for a woman to deliver her people?' she wrote,
citing Esther and Judith as earlier examples. Her followers were
exhorted to 'Come, Come to be the Bride of Christ':

So now then come, as she has done.
Believe My Bible true.
Now as Bride you all shall be.
The Bridegroom all shall know. (5)

To her working-class disciples Joanna brought an ambiguous
message. On the one hand, she echoed the ancient demands of the
disinherited:

But now the heirs I mean to free
And all these bondsmen I'll cast out,
And the true heirs have nought to doubt;
For I'll cut off the bastard race,
And in their stead the true heirs place
For to possess that very land. (6)

And brought a woman's curse on those who conspired to raise the
price of bread, 'My charges will come heavy against them, and my
judgements must be great in the land, if they starve the poor in the
midst of plenty.' (7) But she also devoted a tract to an attack on
Paine which was probably inspired by discussions with some of her
wealthier backers.

Hers was not a revolutionary chiliasm; there was no hint in her
writings of utopian social schemes such as those developed by
another female Messiah of the same period, Ann Lee of the Shakers.
And her writings to her female disciples carried no explicitly
emancipatory message; rather, her language abounded in images of
male villainy and female defiance which aroused women to an anticipation of greater glory. As one of her female followers put it
rather primly one hundred years later: 'The Lord has marvellously
raised the position of women at the end, by thus giving to the world
through Her, His prophecies of things to come.' (8) But the Lord
also assisted Joanna in the rather less cosmic but far more satis-
hying task of defying the male sex. In her writings, Satan was
castigated as 'the liar', the 'betrayer of women' who, when he was
not masquerading as a serpent, was busy philandering with innocent
girls. Joanna had had bitter personal experience of Satan's little
ways: one lover, a man called Saunders, had been revealed as the
seducer of a young woman to whom he had given an abortive herb -
savine - which had killed both herself and her unborn child; (9)
another, a married man called Wills, professed love for Joanna only
to abandon her for his adulterous wife. And it was after Wills's
betrayal that Joanna felt the Eternal Spirit rising within her:

The type of Wills goes deep
For just like he 10,000 be,
And so their end will break. (10)

So goes one of her many prophetic poems; and in an account of her
dispute with Satan - held in a barn over a seven-day period - the
devil revealed a number of recognisably masculine prejudices when,
exasperated with Joanna's verbal abilities, he harangued her for
being a 'damned Bitch' who should learn to hold her waspish tongue.

'It is better to dispute with 1,000 men than one woman', he was said
to complain, finally exploding, 'O, thou bitch of hell! Call me no
more the woman's friend; I hate the sex.' (11) Joanna's reply was
fierce:

> If man can't tame a woman's tongue, how shall the devil? If God
> hath done something to choose a woman to dispute with Satan at
> last, Satan did something to dispute with the woman at first; if
> Satan down-argued the woman at first, she ought to down-argue him
> at last. If Satan scarce gave the woman room to speak or think
> at first, the Woman ought not to give him room to speak or think
> at last.... If Satan paid no regard to the weakness and igno-
> rance of the Woman at first, the weakness and ignorance of the
> Woman will pay no regard to him at last. If he took advantage
> of her weakness, she will take advantage of her strength. If the
> Woman's fall has tired Men, I hope it will tire the Devil also.
> If a Devil could not shame her at first, how shall he shame her
> at last? ... For he glorieth in what the woman doeth that is
> wrong; so IF THE WOMAN IS NOT ASHAMED OF HERSELF, THE DEVIL
> CANNOT SHAME HER!

Satan vanquished, the unity of the Bride and Bridegroom marked
the beginning of a new age, the New Jerusalem:

> Then see ye plain, ye sons of men,
> The way I've led all on.
> It was to Woman, not to Man,
> I in this power did come. (12)

> So Woman here in Love Appear
> You'll find my Love is strong
> To free you all from Adam's Fall.
> If Eve brought in the first,
> Of sorrow here that did appear
> Then I'll bring in the Last;
> For Joy shall come the same to Man;
> So now the WOMAN see!
> MY CHURCH upon HER it must stand,
> AS WOMAN joined with ME. (13)

In 1813, after numerous missionary tours around the country and the
publication of over sixty volumes of prophetic writing, Joanna was
told by her Voices that the Bride was soon to give birth to Shiloh,
the new Messiah. Her poem on this occasion celebrated the unique
mission of womankind:

> Woman brought to Man the GOOD Fruit at the first,
> And from the Woman shall the good Fruit burst ...
> Because no Fruit did ever come from Man
> Though it is often grafted by his Hand. (14)

The Voices commanded her to prepare to wed. And although Joanna
wrote, 'I looked upon matrimony as worse than death', (15) she did
write to a certain Mr Pomeroy to whom she had made such a propo-
sition before. Spurned by him once again, she married a disciple.
In 1814 she had an hysterical pregnancy and died, leaving her
followers to dispute the implications of the tragedy and to await
Shiloh's later arrival.

It is an extraordinary story, made only the more so by the ordi-
nariness of the woman at its centre. Joanna Southcott would have

known nothing of Mary Wollstonecraft; the milieu in which feminist
social critique was developing in the late eighteenth century was
one from which a Devon peasant woman was barred by poverty and ignorance. It is only with the development of the working-class
movements of the early nineteenth century, as we shall see, that
feminist doctrines began to be expressed by working-class women
themselves. None the less, it was the same climate of revolutionary
change which inspired Wollstonecraft's 'Vindication' that also produced the widespread tension, the anticipation of apocalypse, which
was the seed-bed in which Southcottian eschatology flourished.
Throughout the events of the 1790s and early 1800s - revolution just
across the Channel, home-grown Jacobin insurrectionist schemes,
State repression, war and depression - there was created among many
working-class men and women a new sense of actively participating in
a struggle for social advance; conversely, however, there were many
who felt their lives to have been caught up on a tidal wave of
change which they had no hope of directing, except - possibly -
through the grace of God. The oscillation between intense political
activity and chiliastic fervour in this period which E.P.Thompson
has noted, (16) reflected the complexity of people's social experience: what might be lived as an exhilarating development of political power in one year could become fearful anticipation of the advance of the Anti-Christ in a year marked by hunger and defeat.

But these styles of reaction - political radicalism and religious
excitement - were not antithetical. Historians who have hastened to
distinguish the mystical enthusiasm of the Southcottians from the
presumably more tough-minded reformism of those who were, after all,
the forefathers/mothers of modern labour organisation, have employed
too narrow a definition of radical consciousness. And in so doing
they have tended either to ignore the evidence of the interpenetration of heretical religion into early working-class movements or,
where this evidence is too obvious to be ignored, have represented
such an interpenetration as a decline of labour politics into mere
sectarianism, a slip backwards into archaic ideological exotica.
The possibility that religious heresy was itself a weapon of ideological subversion does not seem to have been raised, nor have the
heretical doctrines themselves been read seriously in order to hear
again what they might have had to say to the experience of working-
class disciples.

Any examination of the relationship of women both to heretical
and radical movements forces a consideration of such questions. In
the centuries before Joanna feminist doctrines were frequently articulated in the language of spiritual mission. The heresy of the
female Saviour arose in the Civil War sects of the seventeenth
century, sects in which progressive political ideas and heretical
scriptural interpretation were one and the same, and in which women
frequently employed the rhetoric of spiritual democracy as a basis
on which to challenge patriarchal authority within family, church,
and political life. (17) Then the heresy arose again with the political turbulence of the late eighteenth century: women such as
Betty Gray, 'The Whore of Babylon', (18) Ann Lee, Luckie Buchan in
Scotland, and Joanna Southcott preached to women faced with the
social impact of industrialisation. This later period was generally
one of intense revivalist activity: Methodism expanded six times in

a fifty-year period, fissioning to produce new sects more adequate to the experience of its working-class membership; chiliastic cults continued to flourish, particularly in the north. (19)

Radicalism which developed during Southcott's time was often profoundly marked by the overwhelming dominance of religious thought: even the anti-clerical or atheistic stance taken by many radicals frequently led them not to secular politics, but to schism - to the creation of churches which would more adequately reflect their social beliefs. (20) And when the women involved in these movements spoke of their own claims to power, they used a language which owed more to the Bible than to Wollstonecraft: when the radical women of Lancashire, for example, felt forced to defend their active role in the struggles of 1819 they told their menfolk to go away and look in the Good Book, for 'there you will see that women have been proved the strongest, and that above all things they beareth the victory'. (21)

Radical consciousness in women such as these was not confined to explicit and articulated goals of reform; women, then as now, did not experience their oppression solely in terms of discrimination or poverty or brutality, but also as sexual and intellectual victims of unconscious archetypes, as the subjects of a mental order whose structures of dominance and subordination were internalised in ways that the organised expression of grievances often did not touch, much less challenge in self-conscious struggle. But a sense of grievance and injustice existed none the less, to surface in moments of defiant self-assertion such as those which we hear in the poetry of Southcott. And in the period of rapidly developing radical consciousness in which Southcottianism existed, such moments could be built upon to create a style of feminist rhetoric which flowed into social movements involving women.

It is this process - the transmission of the doctrine of female messianism into the feminism of the women of the first English socialist movement, and the changes which the doctrine underwent as it entered into the ideological struggles of the 1830s and 1840s - which the rest of this essay will examine.

In the years immediately following Joanna's death a number of men and women appeared on public platforms claiming to be the bearers of her mission. These included Joseph Allman, who preached the doctrine of the Woman-God, 'the great, living, life-giving Divine World Mother', George Turner, who 'wed' 1,500 women to Christ and prophesied 'those who are not worth a penny now must be lords of the land. No rents must be paid. No postages for letters.... No taxes', and a Mrs Vaughan, daughter of a prominent Jacobin. (22) Even during Joanna's lifetime she had had female competitors, particularly Mary Bateman, a Leeds abortionist who having had a brisk practice in spells and curses, acquired one of Joanna's seals and decided to turn her hand to Redemption. She declared herself the preacher of the New Revelation, and to any who remained sceptical she would show eggs laid by her hens inscribed 'CRIST (sic) IS COMING'.

The first evidence of contact between Southcottian prophets and working-class radicals is in the 1830s, when several Joannaites arrived on the London radical scene. One of these was a shoemaker,

Zion Ward, who believed himself to be Joanna's Shiloh. He had originally been taught his Southcottianism by Mary Boon, another Devon peasant prophetess, but as he made contact with the republi- canism and anti-clericalism of radicals such as Richard Carlile, his preaching became more attuned to the anti-Establishment sentiments of his London plebeian audiences. His attacks on the clergy - the 'scurvy nincompoops' led by 'His Grease' the Archbishop - were de- livered in combination with several other popular radical themes, including schemes for utopian social communities and a libertarian sexual morality: 'if you love one another, go together at any time without law or ceremony.' (24)

Ward preached in the radical working-class centre, the Rotunda, in 1831. The following year he was imprisoned for blasphemy. But his place was quickly taken by another young Southcottian just arrived from the north, the Reverend James Elishma Smith. (25) Smith was a young Edinburgh man who had been trained for the Presby- terian ministry, but was continually drawn to seek more exciting theological pastures; upon completing his training he had become a follower of the millennialist Edward Irving, but after discovering Southcottian doctrine - again through the teachings of an old woman - he travelled to join the sect in Ashton-under-Lyne. (26) Ashton in the 1830s was a very militant centre of radical politics, and the period which Smith spent with the Southcottians there may well have taught him more than the intricacies of Joannaite eschatological doctrine; at any rate, very soon after his arrival in London he was drawing large audiences of radicals to his regular lectures. In particular he became a focus of interest for a growing body of radi- cals in the metropolis, the followers of Robert Owen.

The Owenites, or 'co-operators' as they were called in the early 1830s, were mainly male and female working-class radicals committed to the establishment of 'communities of mutual co-operation' based on social production, common property, and a loving disposition of each to her/his neighbour. Since 1824 Robert Owen had been in the USA spending the profits of his earlier cotton enterprise at New Lanark in an attempt to establish such communities, and in this period the working-class leaders who had originally been contemptu- ous of Owen's philanthropic paternalism began to develop some of his ideas in accordance with their own progressive aspirations. A whole panoply of reformist schemes developed, ranging from worker-con- trolled educational programmes and co-operative shops to communities in England and Ireland. (27)

Women were involved in all these projects, and the rhetoric of Owenite co-operation was explicitly feminist. In 1825 two of the leading advocates of communitarian reform, William Thompson and Anna Wheeler, published their 'Appeal of one half the Human Race, Women, against the pretensions of the other Half, Men, to retain them in Civil and Domestic Slavery' in which they demanded equality for women in all spheres - education, marriage, political life. In the same year the London Co-Operative Society's published plan for the establishment of a social community stated as one of its central objects the eradication of all forms of sexual inequality; (28) letters and articles in the various Owenite newspapers developed this theme in discussions of co-operative housekeeping in community, abolition of male marriage privileges, the role of women in radical political organisation. (29)

The London in which Smith arrived, then, was buzzing with projects involving female co-operators: women attending radical schools and lectures, holding 'Social' tea parties for the cause, sewing for the Labour Exchanges (Owen's institutions where workers could exchange their products for other goods at a rate determined by the value of their labour time), arguing their position in the meetings which planned new communities. By 1832 these women were also becoming very active in the new trade unions.

A glance at a page of the Owenite newspaper, 'The Crisis', gives the flavour of this new radicalism among women: much of the page is given over to a report of a lecture delivered by a woman called Mrs Hamilton to 'a crowded audience of both sexes' in Paisley,

The established church, or, as she quaintly denominated it, 'the old Lady' came in for a principal share of her vituperation - a course of proceeding which, she says, she finds highly useful in opening the doors of the voluntary churches in many parts of the country. The 'reformation' of her own sex she declares to be one of the grand objects of her labours. She complained loudly, and in no very delicate terms, of the tyranny with which males lorded it over females, and advised the latter to be ruled no longer. In handling this part of the subject she said the apostles were taught to become fishers of men, and (shaking her fist towards the women) she added, 'I will teach you how to become fishers of men' - a sentiment which elicited great laughter and applause.

There was more in this vein, to be followed the next day by a lecture in which she used the findings of phrenology (the study of personality based on the topology of the skull) to argue that 'women's brains were capable of being improved to a degree which would make them equal ... and give them power to break the chains of the tyrant and the oppressor and set them completely free. (Immense applause.)'

The same newspaper page also carried a short report on a meeting of 'shipwrights, ship-joiners, caulkers, smiths, and others' in which a resolution in support of a 'general union of all trades' was passed, an announcement of the establishment of the Female Lodge of the Surrey Miscellaneous Trades Lodge, advertisements for Social Festivals and Tea Parties at the Owenite Institution on Charlotte Street and one for a free public discussion on the topic 'Why are the Working Classes, who produce all the wealth in the world, in poverty and misery?', and the conclusion of an article by a woman who, after listing all the social disabilities of womankind in modern society, demanded: 'When, therefore, all these things, and many more equally unjust and injurious towards women, are considered, who amongst them will not exclaim with Lady Macbeth "unsex me!".' (30) It is a mixture peculiar to modern eyes, unused as we are to the presence of militant feminism in labour organisation. Radical women of the early nineteenth century were drawn largely from two sectors of the population: the artisan layer of the working class and the women of impoverished gentility of the lower middle class. For the women of the first sector, craft workers and their families, the early nineteenth century was a time of change which was both frightening and exciting, as well as a period of great hardship for many of them. Workers in the old crafts - shoemakers, tailors, etc. - faced the erosion of skilled labour under the dual impact of machinery and sweating;   wage rates fell in most trades;   enclosure and urbanisation brought increasing numbers of depressed workers into these over-stocked trades to accelerate de-skilling and underpayment even more. (31)   Women were a key source of labour for these changes, both as new machine workers and as cheap labour in the sweated trades.   Their intense exploitation (and that of their children) was felt by the entire working class to be one of the most degrading and oppressive features of the new order based on machinery and administered by political economy;   the involvement of women themselves in the new radical organisations was a response both to new hardships and the sense of new possibilities in a 'world turned upside down'.   'I am induced to plead to the men, from hearing so many say they do not like women from home' wrote a bonnet-maker in one letter to a radical newspaper advocating women's unions, 'are we not forced from home to labour, and may we not go from home to endeavour to lighten that labour, without the fear of an angry husband when we return? ... Let us, sister workwomen, make a beginning in our own business;   our number is great, our power equal.' (32)

In 1832 a number of articles appeared in 'The Crisis' taking up feminist and trade unionist issues and linking them to a discussion of the heresy of the female Messiah.   These were written by Smith, who in 1833 became editor of the newspaper, a position which he used as a platform to promote a combination of sophisticated class strategy (he was one of the earliest advocates of industrial syndicalism) and millennialist prophecy.   His feminism had this two-sided quality: thus in one editorial he delivered a sharp comment on the attitude of certain male trade unionists to the women's unions - 'are not the women one-half of humanity?   Are they not fellow-labourers.... Are they not more oppressed, and more inequitably paid, than their more robust partners?' (33) - while in another place developing his views on the Age of the Bride:

In the religious world we ... look for what are commonly called hallucinations in women, calling themselves the bride, professing to be called of God.... These are not imposters, but forerunners of a great change of system ... (a change which has been) taught in the school of faith and in the school of infidelity ... the one setting forth woman as the mother of Messiah, and the other laying claim to the equality of woman, and her emancipation from thraldom. (34)

In another article on the history of the heresy he wrote that 'believers in modern prophecy differ in their opinions of this free woman who is coming ... but many say she will put an end to marriage, and introduce an entirely new era in the social and domestic system.' (35)   In his own newspaper, 'The Shepherd', begun in 1835 after he left 'The Crisis' over disagreements with Owen, Smith developed the Doctrine of the Woman in a series of articles in which he elaborated a 'universalist' cosmology.   According to this theory, Nature was a self-transforming unity whose twin principles of motion are the male/spiritual and female/material.

The positive and negative forces seek each other.... Hence it follows that man, who represents the spiritual, holds the material sword; but woman, representing the material, has the moral power, which will ultimately overcome the former.   Woman is a

refinement of man ... she is the end of the old world and the new
can only begin with her complete emancipation from the curse of
the first. (36)

In his 1833 'Lecture on a Christian Community' Smith argued that th
this emancipatory mission of women could only be realised within a
communist society, depicted as one of elegance, music, liberal education for both sexes, and romantic relationships inspired by
'natural affection' rather than economic necessity. Feminist
religions must have feminist paradises. In developing this link
between the doctrine of the female Messiah and the project of social
community, Smith was influenced not only by his Southcottian
background and his Owenite activities, but also by yet another
radical grouping: the French utopian socialists. Soon after his
arrival in London, he had become friendly with Anna Wheeler who had
spent some time with the followers of Henri de Saint-Simon in Caen
in 1818. Through her Smith became aware of the Saint-Simonians'
programme for the joint emancipation of women and the working class;
as editor of 'The Crisis' he published Wheeler's translations of
articles from the women's Saint-Simonian journal, 'Tribune des
Femmes'. (37)

Here our story of the influence of Southcottianism on Owenite
feminism must take a short detour through the French doctrine of
'La Femme Libre'. The story of the Saint-Simonian sojourn into
English radical politics is a fascinating example of the cross-
fertilisation of heretical feminist doctrine in this period. (38)
In 1832, seven years after Saint-Simon's death, a number of
'missionaries' arrived in London at the invitation of men such as
Thomas Carlyle and J.S.Mill. But these eminent enthusiasts soon
became disillusioned, and the French socialists found their most
receptive audiences among the Owenites, particularly among the
Owenite women. As one enthusiastic missionary reported to the
leader of the movement in Paris, 'Père' Enfantin,

At the gatherings which I attended (of Owen's disciples) I saw a
large number of women on the platform. I have seldom seen faces
so animated as theirs. They felt their equality with men ...
there are a number ... who are noted for their writings and
lectures. (39)

The Saint-Simonian feminists, like the Owenites, lectured on a range
of issues of concern to women, from easier access to divorce to the
phrenological evidence for female intellectual equality. Anna
Wheeler delivered lectures on women's rights at Saint-Simonian
meetings in London, as did another well-known feminist and
freethinker, Eliza Macaulay, a woman called Mrs Emery, and one
simply called 'a London Mechanic's wife'. (40) Saint-Simonian women
were reported in the working-class press as lecturing in provincial
centres in 1833, and in that year twice-weekly meetings on women's
emancipation were held in Owen's Burton-rooms in London, (41) where
another anti-clerical feminist, Eliza Sharples, also lectured. (42)

In 1834 the two leading London missionaries published a manifesto
in which it was stated

we proclaim the advent of the Mother ... the advent of a new
Church, wherein the spirit of emancipated women will unfold its
germs of moral feelings and be instrumental in building up the
new heaven and the new earth. (43)

Saint-Simon bore no responsibility for this doctrine. In the years after his death, his disciple Enfantin announced that the arrival of the New Jerusalem was to be heralded by the establishment of the androgynous godhead whose material manifestation was the unity of the 'Père' himself with his High Priestess, the female Messiah. Thanks to a message received by two girls in a hypnotic trance, a number of the faithful hurried off to Constantinople to seek out 'La Mère', and reports on the progress of these emissaries were delivered in London meetings.

That a feminist sect developing in a nation who religious mentality was dominated by the image of a Virgin Mother should produce an attenuated version of this image to express emancipatory aspirations is, perhaps, not so surprising; what is fascinating is to catch a glimpse of whatever heretical traditions in the lives of English women might have caused this doctrine to resonate sympathetically among some of them. In November 1833 'The Times' carried an account of a London meeting which gives such a glimpse: the meeting, which was described as 'chiefly composed of the followers of Mr Owen', including female followers, was opened by Fontana, the chief Saint-Simonian missionary, who introduced the English radical Rowland Detrosier. Detrosier then read letters from a number of the faithful search for 'La Mère' in Constantinople; when he described the doctrine of the Mother a number of the women present are recorded as cheering. The only dissenting voice was that of a woman who rose to argue that they should follow their own female Messiah, Joanna Southcott; when she sat down a young Owenite rose to say

> he thought it a matter of gratification to see a woman rise to
> declare her sentiments in a public meeting. He knew many
> Southcotians (sic) and as their social views were much in unison
> with their (the Owenites) own, he did not see that it mattered
> whether the cause was the spirit or man's reason, provided the
> glorious result was obtained. (Hear, hear.) (44)

How are we to interpret such an occasion? The unity of human reason and the religious spirit postulated in the speech of the young Owenite was a central tenet of socialist thought. Moral and political categories were inseparable in this ideology, drawing as it did upon traditions whose religious nature consisted less, perhaps, in the espousal of one or other body of theological doctrine than in this very commitment to the fusion of the visionary and the practical. Even the most anti-clerical of the Owenite feminists propagandised socialism as a 'new moral world' as well as a strategy for women's social advance: Emma Martin, for example, was one well-known 'infidel' lecturess in the movement who combined virulent attacks on the established church with lectures on 'Socialism, the one True Religion'; on one occasion she lectured on 'The Holy Ghost: HER Nature, Offices and Laws' (45) and on another concluded a discussion of women's rights under Socialism with the following:

> One great evil is, the depraved and ignorant condition of woman;
> this evil can only be removed by Socialism. We love Socialism,
> because it is more moral - we love Socialism, because it is more
> benevolent - we love Socialism, because it is the only universal
> system of deliverance that man and woman can adopt. (46)

In other talks, she promised to her female listeners a socialism of faithful husbands, well-fed children, co-operative housework, but -

above all - a life of personal dignity and intellectual enlighten-
ment. In communitarian life women would be accorded the respect
denied them elsewhere, their true social value would finally be
recognised.

The importance of this appeal to women's pride and self-assertion
is evident in all the feminist writings of the period; it links
Southcott to Wollstonecraft and both to working women such as those
we have been discussing. We can hear it in this letter from 'A
Female Socialist' in which the writer had some sharp words for a
clerical opponent of socialism who had referred to the female reformers at a political meeting as 'poor, silly women':

> for, if some of them could have summoned courage to reply to
> him ... he would not have found them quite so silly as he wished
> to make them appear ... I hope my fellow females will rouse all
> their energies, and let the priesthood see that we have moral
> courage to depend upon our own exertions, with the confidence
> that the God who made us, is both able and willing to make us
> happy, without their canting, hypocritical nonsense; and as
> woman is said to have been first in the transgression, let it
> not be said that she is last in promoting the regeneration of
> mankind. (47)

The path of God's true believers, it was argued, is the road to
socialism and women's emancipation. A letter to 'The Pioneer' from
an Owenite tailoress stated that God made Eve out of Adam's rib to
show not that she was inferior, but that she was essential to his
existence, was his equal. (48) And the Sacred Socialist, John
Finch, wrote that it could be 'abundantly proved from the sayings
of Christ' that 'He had dictated no creed, enjoined no sabbath ...
allowed no artificial distinctions of higher and lower classes, nor
gave any pre-eminence of the one sex of the human race over another.' (49)

We have moved, then, from examining the relationship between
radical ideologies and the impulses toward female self-assertion
expressed in a heretical church - Southcottianism - to the con-
jecture which is the reverse side of the argument: to what extent
was the involvement of women in the self-consciously feminist
politics of the Owenite movement an attempt to found a religion
which would be both culturally and ideologically adequate to women's
emancipatory purpose? Southcott herself had been an active Methodist before the revelation of her messianic mission, and this at a
time when the ministry of women in the Connexion was under official
attack. She even took the message of her Voices to her local class
meeting, only to be jeered down. Emma Martin and another feminist
lecturer, Margaret Chappellsmith, had both been very active in dissenting churches before their conversion to socialism, and Emma had
been a feminist before leaving her church (deserting her husband at
the same time). (50) In the years after the collapse of the general
union of 1834 the Owenite movement deliberately adopted a structure
of organisation modelled on the Methodist Connexion, including a
Social Bible and Social Hymns, developed its own rituals around
birth, marriage and death, and created a style of social life which
closely resembled that of plebeian congregations. How are we to
interpret this style of radical and feminist politics?

It has been argued by at least one historian of the Owenite
movement that after 1835 Owenism became a millennialist sect:

Except for a brief period of a few months in 1833-34 when Owen
put himself at the head of a mass trade union movement in
Britain, the Owenites were a millennarian sect, using the term
in its general sense of a small religious group, in which
membership is voluntary and limited to persons having certain
special convictions or experiences in common. A rejection of the
values of society, and withdrawal or separateness from the world,
together with an expectation of adventism further typify the
sect. A mission to preach the kingdom, an emphasis on fellowship
... and allegiance understood as 'belief in the truth' are also
commonly found. (51)

I think it is probably true that the women who became Owenite
socialists were drawn to the movement by some of the same impulses
which drew women to Southcottianism. But I have also tried to
indicate the ways in which these impulses, far from being disengaged
from social values, were defiant - an assertion of female power and
equality in the face of prevailing hostility to any improvement in
women's role. Southcott's vision of feminine aggrandisement may
have laid fertile mental ground in which socialist feminist
doctrines could be sown, although to show this one would require
much more evidence than I have of interpenetrating memberships of
Southcottian sects and Owenite branches. But if Southcott's
preaching can be interpreted, in part, as a protest against masculine power, it offered women no more than the catharsis of defiance
and the hope of millennium, whereas socialist feminism offered a
careful programme for social change. And this programme, far from
being one of 'withdrawal from the world', was intensely combative.
Even the goal - independent communities - was not seen as an end in
itself but a means to a project of world reform which would require
continuous propaganda, endless confrontation with the forces of
institutionalised 'error'.

Inasmuch as certain millennialist heresies - such as the doctrine
of the female Messiah - became part of this propaganda, they became
weapons to be wielded by men and women in a battle which was as much
one of the imagination as of meeting-halls and streets. Nothing
could be further from the truth than to regard socialist feminism as
one more eccentricity of an inward-looking sect; it was developed
in the heat of ideological battle. It is this battle, and the ways
in which the heretical Doctrine of the Woman was shaped by it, which
is now described. But in order to do so, we will look away from the
Owenite movement as a whole to a detailed examination of one
grouping within it, the Communist Church, and their doctrine of the
'Woman-Power'.

Woman-Saviour now we muster
To await thy advent sure,
In the cluster of thy lustre,
Come and leave the earth no more?
Then before thy gentle look,
Swords shall quail and warriors fail,
And the spear, a shepherd's crook,
Shall adorn the daisied dale.
Woman-power! Incarnate Love!

Human Goddess come and be,
If the Bridegroom's tears can move,
Bride unto Humanity.
Thou alone of all can save us
Let us be what thou would have us! (52)

Between 1835 and 1840 a series of articles appeared in the Owenite newspaper, 'The New Moral World', under the pseudonym 'Kate'. While the themes developed in them were fairly typical of middle-class feminism - women's right to education, proposals for reform of marriage laws, and so on - there were also indications of a more radical approach: private property was condemned as the source of male power; class differences were explored, and a social morality based on 'family interests' was condemned not only as selfish and competitive but also as irrelevant to the lives of the mass of property-less workers. In the upper classes, Kate pointed out, a woman may lose her child in divorce (this was at the time of the Caroline Norton case) while in the working classes the mother

> destitute of food and shelter, and, with these, of everything
> that can render the society of her child aught but a torture, is
> commanded to fulfill her maternal duties.... What mockery, then,
> for man to talk of consideration of women's delicacy of nerves
> and feelings. (53)

The author of these articles was a young woman named Catherine Watkins. I have been unable so far to discover anything about Kate's life prior to her involvement in the socialist movement. It seems likely, however, that she was from the sort of lower middle-class or trades background which was referred to above as a second source of Owenite feminists; in particular, her proposal that any decline in employment opportunities for women should be remedied by increasing their shop and office employment indicates that she mixed with the young professional and non-manual workers of London whose claims to middle-class status were insecure at best. The women of this sector were in a particularly precarious position in this period: for them unmarried status often meant a quick decline from a comfortable, if cloying, gentility, to the genteel poverty of governessing, teaching, shop-assisting, needlework, or - as in the case of several socialist feminists, including Kate - badly paid literary activities. Many such young women, and their 'black-coated worker' male counterparts, were radicals, although more often political Radicals rather than Socialists, socialism being so clearly identified in the public mind with the infidelity and immorality of the lower orders.

John Goodwyn Barmby came from such a background. (54) His father had been a Suffolk solicitor, he was well educated, and a radical from the start. At sixteen Goodwyn could be found haranguing groups of local agricultural labourers on the inequities of the new Poor Law; by his early twenties he, like Kate, had turned to radical journalism, writing long articles for the 'New Moral World' on the doctrinal differences between Fourierism and Owenism, on socialism and medical theory, on evolution. (55) He also wrote for 'The New Age', the journal of the Ham Common Concordium, a socialist community which had been established by a Southcottian, Charles Lane, and J.P.Greaves, a follower of Zion Ward. During 1840 Barmby spent some time in Paris, where he familiarised himself with French and German socialism and became very friendly with the French feminist Flora Tristan. (56) He was a good internationalist, keeping touch with Cabet and Weitling and Friedrich Engels throughout the 1840s. It seems likely that it was also in 1840 that he met Kate.

In April of that year Kate wrote to the 'New Moral World' praising the feminism of the socialists, and in particular their 'moral courage' in 'furnishing society with the better example' of treating men and women as equals in all social functions. (57) It was possibly at one such function, perhaps a Social Festival where food and dancing compensated for the inevitable long-winded speech from Owen, that Kate and Goodwyn met. We may imagine each impressing the other with the quality of their social views. At any rate, in 1841 they began to work together to establish a distinct grouping within the movement, the 'communist school of social reformers' whose organisation was the 'Central Communist Propaganda Society'. An early article in the organisation's newspaper combined the usual anti-clericalism of Owenism with its own brand of chiliastic prophecy:

> The parson is feasting with the peer upon ... turbot, while the
> poor man is starving at his gate. The tyrant is taxing the unrepresented, and tything the uninstructed. All things are in a
> state of practical infidelity and material atheism. The world
> is heaving as with the throes of a woman with child, and a new
> faith, a new religion, must be born unto the people ... it must
> be Communism. (58)

The new organisation quickly developed its own mini-version of the movement's branch structure based on groups in Cheltenham, Ipswich, Merthyr Tydfil, Strabane in Ireland, and London. A Communist Temple was established at the Circus, Great Marylebone, and by the end of 1841 regular lectures were being delivered here and in the provincial centres. Their first newspaper, 'The Educational Circular', quickly gained a circulation of one thousand, which was respectably high for the time. (59) Members of the Communist Society joined the official 'Social Missionaries' of the Owenite movement (now called the Rational Society) in touring the country speaking on women's suffrage, marriage and divorce, Socialism vs Chartism, and other topics of societarian interest. Emma Martin presided over a Communist meeting on marriage, (60) and one of the Communists was the medical officer for the Owenite community in Hampshire, (61) so it seems likely that the new organisation remained pretty much under the umbrella of the Owenite movement.

The Communist Church was founded at the height of the organised strength of the socialist movement, and also at the point of the most intensive anti-socialist campaigning on the part of church and government. In 1840 the Bishop of Exeter delivered a speech in the House of Lords in which he chilled blue blood with a delineation of the socialist programme of immorality and atheism. There were, he told the House, sixty-one branches of the movement across the country, each of which was in one of fourteen districts to which a Social Missionary was attached. There was an Executive Committee responsible for the publication of thousands of subversive tracts and a newspaper, the 'New Moral World', whose readership he estimated at 400,000. After quoting from Owen's lectures on marriage - an anti-clerical polemic in favour of 'unions of Nature' un-

trammelled by priestly or legal sanction - and threatening to quote
from Owen's son's tract on birth control, he offered a number of
spicy anecdotes on the home life of well-known socialists. He
summed up,

> The state of things is dangerous: the open defiance of God ...
> which occurred in the paid lectures of this society, were abso-
> lutely horrid. He had even heard more than one instance of a
> female lecturer, not absolutely defying her Maker, but putting
> forth all the horrid and abominable pollutions of this society.
> (62)

It is within the context of this hostility that the feminism of
the Owenites and the Communist Church must be understood. By 1840-1
not only a number of female lecturers but also many rank and file
women socialists were entering into the fray with verve. The issue
of marriage reform - easy access to divorce, sexual equality in
marriage, abolition of church control over marriage - was a key
battleground in what one Owenite called 'this war of ideas' of the
1840s; the flavour of the debate from the feminist side was caught
in a letter written by a woman who lived in an Owenite community in
Cambridgeshire to the community's newspaper:

> Of what utility is the mummery of priest or lawyer? Why should
> sexual connexions be more fettered than hunger or thirst?
> Mr Owen has often said we cannot pledge to love for twenty-four
> hours. If we cannot love as we like, why attempt to bind parties
> together who do not mutually love? ... A time is fast ap-
> proaching when this important subject must be fairly met ...
> woman, abused, ill-treated woman must ere long be placed upon an
> equality with man, and love of the most disinterested nature be
> experienced by both sexes. (63)

When one of the socialist feminists lectured on marriage thousands
of men and women turned out to hear; debates on the issue between
a socialist and a clerical opponent became spectacles in which
attack and counter-attack was accompanied by the cheering, heckling
and feet-stamping of crowds of up to 5,000. (64) Tracts produced by
socialists on this and other subjects were met by a barrage of
tracts issued by religious opponents: a typical oppositional tract
was one which described socialist communities as brothels where 'all
are to yield themselves up to be governed by the unrestrained
instincts of nature, in imitation of dogs and goats'. (65)
Newspapers such as 'Fraser's Magazine' prophesied the downfall of
Christian society through the corruption of its womanhood by socialist propaganda; (66) City missionaries preached sermons in which
they implored women not to marry socialists; (67) the press
frequently reported cases of wife-desertion or wife-beating as
'Incidences of Socialism'; (68) female socialists were described
in publications as 'whores' and 'libidinous in mind and body'; (69)
petitions against socialism were circulated in many towns, demanding
it be suppressed as a blasphemous and hence seditious organisation.
All of this had its effect in creating hostility and fear: socialist halls were vandalised and burnt, lecturers mobbed and beaten,
hundreds of socialists were sacked by employers who on several occasions broke into meetings to see if any of their workers were
present; female socialists were chased and stoned in a number of
cities, on one occasion the crowd jeering 'Are you her with the

seven husbands?' (70) Riots occurred involving versions of 'Church
and King' mobs who were sometimes known to have been encouraged by
local clergy or government officials. And in Stockport a little
girl who preached socialism to her schoolmates was summarily ex-
pelled. (71)

Evangelical ladies also joined in the attack. During the same
period as a feminist consciousness was developing among radical
women, evangelicals such as Sarah Lewis and Charlotte Elizabeth
Tonna were writing reams of abysmal prose on the power of women's
'moral influence' which was to transfigure social life through the
inculcation of religious and domestic principles in the sons of
pious mothers. 'The one quality upon which women's value and influence depends is the renunciation of self' (72) wrote Sarah Lewis,
while Charlotte Elizabeth reminded her readers of the Eve in every
woman: 'One painful preeminence women cannot deny to be ours, for
"the woman was the first in the transgression" ... with this sad
proof of her extreme instability before us, we had better refrain
from speculating on the subject of her supposed equality with men.'
(73) For women such as Charlotte Elizabeth, the feminism of the
socialists was further damning evidence of immoralism and atheism.
Her journal 'The Christian Lady's Magazine' bewailed the popularity
of Owenite lectures among 'the humbler ranks of society'. 'Hundreds
of rooms re-echo every night ... to such blasphemies as were never
heard ... while crowds of English females applaud them.' Her description of the socialist doctrines was typical of the religious
opposition:

the main plan is, first, to wholly abolish marriage....
Secondly, to take every child from its mother, at the time of
its birth ... and to commit the infants to persons appointed for
the charge, who shall nourish them like a promiscuous litter of
pigs. Thirdly ... to do away with that sacred and endearing
thing - home.... There is to be no separate dwelling, no
husband, no wife, no parent, no child, no brother, no sister,
no neighbour, no friend, no pastor, NO GOD! (74)

I have described these ideological battles at some length because it
is in this context that heresy and scriptural interpretation became
important weapons for the working class, and for women in particular. The high level of antagonism between existing churches and the
radicals did not necessarily imply secularisation of working-class
progressives. The struggle toward ideological self-definition must
necessarily start in the common vocabulary, but as this struggle
developed the very meaning of words became a site on which it was
played out; the appropriation and subversion of the language of
scripture a key moment in the development of emancipatory ideals.
It is in this way that the language of the millennialist socialists
can be understood, as we shall see now in the texts of the Communist
Church and in particular in their version of the doctrine of the
'Woman-Power'.

In 1841 the 'New Moral World' published an article by Goodwyn
titled 'The Man-Power, the Woman-Power, and the Woman-Man-Power'.
(75) It began

In the times of barbarization and feudalism was the man-power
strong and dominant. Physical force reigned triumphant. Gentleness ruled only secretly in the bosom of woman. Hence we have

learned to term gentleness and its sentiment equations as the
woman-power. Long was it in abeyance to the man-power, or physical empire; but now, at last, it is beginning to prevail. Love
is its God ... and it therefore beams like the sun itself, from
the bosom of the true Socialist, irradiating the heart of every
real communist.

There is then outlined a complicated theory of the evolutionary
progress of the 'humanitarian mass' which is to culminate in a
millennium heralded by the rise of Owenism:

In England is an apostle preaching of the gospel of community,
many are listening, and the woman-power says, in sweet tones,
'Yea, verily,' but the man-power hoarsely shouts ... 'Crucify
him, crucify him!' Yet the woman-power is prevailing and he
lives; nor can the man-power murder him, for he is love, and
love cannot die.

Various diagrams are used to illustrate the historical vacillation
between the forces of man-power and woman-power, demonstrating that
the 'equilibration' is reached in the birth of certain men and women
who contain within themselves both the male and female elements, and
who are hailed as 'the true priests of humanity'. The two examples
which are given are Shelley and Mary Wollstonecraft, and Goodwyn
obviously had himself in mind as a third, with a little note that
'the existence of the woman-power does not necessarily imply that
the man or woman possessing it is endued with what we call effemi-
nateness.' Eventually the entire earth is to be populated by this
new bisexual race, created in socialist communities where a reorganised social environment provides the conditions necessary for
the emergence of the 'Woman-Man-Power'. Goodwyn acknowledges his
debt to Southcott for all this: 'When an enthusiastic woman pro-
claimed the reign of women upon earth, and asserted their future
empire over men, she knew not what she said, but yet she was a
prophetess.' Joanna's error, however, was her identification of the
reign of woman-power with the actual reign of women: 'she saw the
might of gentleness in woman, but knew not that her natures were
really common with those of man, although the better natures of man
were actually dormant.' (None the less, Barmby remained enough of a
disciple to Southcott to make a later attempt to drum up support for
the sect's demand that her Box of prophecies should be opened. (76))
The article concluded on a strongly chiliastic note - 'Let the
Messiah be within us, it will socialize our planet and establish
true communism amid our globe' - which was more than echoed in an
article written by Kate for the 'Educational Circular':

The mission of woman is discovered by Communism: will she hesi-
tate to perform it? The grass is growing, sorrow is accumulating
- waves are rushing, the world is warring - life and death, soul
and body, are in the conflict, the saviour is in the hearts of
the redeemed, the prophet is the inspired one, WOMAN LEARN THY
MISSION? DO IT? AND FEAR NOT? - the world is saved. (77)

The themes developed in Goodwyn and Kate's writing clearly owed much
not only to an adventurous amalgamation of Southcottian-Saint-
Simonian-Romantic influences (many of the themes of Goodwyn's
article, for example, were drawn from Shelley's 'Revolt of Islam',
an account of the misadventures of a young couple on a mission to
redeem mankind, in which the woman is represented as a feminist

saviour of all women) but also to their involvement in the socialist struggle itself. According to the Communists, the feminine principle - the 'woman-power' - is Love, the basis of all libertarian social organisation. Unlike the evangelical authors of the concept of a peculiarly domestic mission for women, the Communists believed that when Love set out to emancipate, it created a social revolution. Love and private property could not co-exist; neither could the loving life be one in which half the human race was without economic power or political rights. The Communists were involved in Chartism as well as Owenism, and the first demand raised by their organisation was for the inclusion of female suffrage in the People's Charter:

> We assert that man and woman are equal each to each. We are opposed to sex legislation as we are opposed to class legislation. We therefore ask by the names of Mary Wolstonecraft (sic) and Charlotte Corday, for universal suffrage ... for unsexual Chartism. (78)

Goodwyn's notion of the psychically androgynous Communist - the 'Man-Woman-Power' has many possible referents: to Southcott's prophesied union of the Bridegroom and Bride, to the heresy of the originally hermaphroditic Adam/Eve, split in the Fall and forever seeking re-unification (Goodwyn commented favourably on this doctrine); to the Saint-Simonians' notion of 'La Femme Libre' and Shelley's version of a similar doctrine; and - more prosaically - to Goodwyn's own marriage to Kate. They appear to have been wed in 1841; an article by Goodwyn was timely: 'I announce love to be the sacred bond of marriage. I declare that two only at the same time can feel that particular love that is completed in marriage. I affirm that divorce begins when love ends.' (79) After an abortive attempt to establish a community at Hanwell, the Communists concentrated on expanding their organised base among working-class radicals. By 1845 there were two groups in London and groups in about a dozen other towns; the organisation was strong enough by this time to prompt one sympathiser to speculate that it might take over the leadership of the socialist movement after the collapse of the official movement community at Queenswood in 1845. (80) While the Church was never centre stage in radical politics, then, nor was it simply a marginal eccentric sect. Its programme included virtually all the popular radical causes of the 1840s, and it publicised these in numerous newspapers and tracts. Goodwyn was a delegate to the Chartist Convention of 1842 representing Suffolk, (81) and appears to have been a parliamentary candidate for Ipswich at one point as well. (82)

For its adherents, then, the Church offered both a utopian faith and a political purpose. It certainly did have its more exotic features, such as an evangelical enthusiasm for vegetarianism, but then so did virtually all early nineteenth century radicalism. And doctrines which may at first appear as mere eccentricities may be revealed to carry much more symbolic importance than is realised. This was true of the many examples of radical re-interpretation of the scriptures, and it was also true of the doctrine of female messianism, of the Woman-Power.

Two documents written by Kate Barmby demonstrate this point clearly. 'The Demand for the Emancipation of Woman' appeared in

1843. (83) It began, as did most feminist tracts, with a quote from
Shelley's 'Queen Mab', and then went on to list three demands: the
political, the domestic, and the ecclesiastical emancipation of
women. It is worth quoting at some length:

> We demand the political emancipation of woman, because it is her
> right ... because she is ... expected to pay the same taxes ...
> and because all other laws act as several, many more severely
> upon her than upon man.... This can only be acquired by her
> possession of the suffrage equally with man.... There is now
> being agitated an electoral document, entitled the PEOPLE'S
> CHARTER, advocating a general masculine suffrage. Women must,
> before they give it their support, insist upon the insertion of
> clauses advocating general feminine suffrage as well....
>
> We demand the domestic emancipation of woman.... We demand
> for her independence in the pursuit of those labours for which
> she is most particularly adapted, and which alone can be her
> security from the tyranny of her husband, and her preservation
> from the oppressions of society. In fine, we demand the emanci-
> pation of the hand of woman from mere household drudgery.... The
> women, the poor women of the working class, with their intelli-
> gence undeveloped, toiling, ever toiling on, are told by men who
> know all the wretchedness of their condition, that home and fire-
> side, duty to their children, and love to their husbands, must be
> the never-failing spring, the bright star to yield them light in
> the darkest darkness! Oh, it is sad to think of the helotage
> which women suffer.

She went on to argue, here and in the second document, an article
titled 'Women's Industrial Independence', (84) that even the jobs
formerly open to women, such as midwifery, were being given over to
men, forcing women into domestic isolation and dependence on their
husbands' wage. In present society 'competition places man in an
antagonistic position to women in the labour market'; it is only
with the establishment of a communist society 'with its associative
household, with its common nursery, and with its organisation of
industry adapted for both sexes' that women's independence can be
assured.

In the struggle to achieve emancipation, Kate argued, women must
look to the men of the working class for support, and 'should they
not at once perceive the justice of her demand, it will prove indeed
that evil example worketh much mischief' for they would be acting to
their sisters as 'the Tories have evilly acted toward them'. She
had no patience with doctrines of forbearance and 'moral influence';
the question for women and the working class as a whole was one of
power.

> it is only a short time since the working men came forward to
> declare their own grievances ... and now if they are not more
> loved by those above them in rank and wealth they certainly are
> more feared by them.

Woman-Power and class power are strategically linked in the struggle
for the 'ecclesiastical emancipation of women', the final demand
which Kate raised in her tract. There must be established a new
holy order, based on community and universal Love:

> The means for effecting the ecclesiastical emancipation of woman
> appear to us to consist in the formation of a 'woman's society'

in every city, town and village possible. In this society women
might converse, discuss, and speak upon their rights, their
wrongs, and their destiny; they might consult upon their own
welfare and that of the great human family, and thus prepare each
other for the mission of the apostle in society at large.

These societies, Kate went on, should agitate for female suffrage as
well as other social demands; and in order that they might enlist
greater support among women, she proposed the establishment of a
national 'Woman's Magazine', a proposal which presumably would have
had great appeal for the many indigent radical feminist journalists
of the 1840s.

In the propaganda of the Communist Church, and particularly in the
writing of Kate Barmby, we can see how the doctrine of the female
Messiah became a rallying-cry for a women's struggle to gain social
and political rights. In the context of the socialist struggles of
the 1840s, women's demands gained a greater urgency than before, and
the heresy which in Southcott's poetry expressed an untheorised
impulse toward power was able to emerge as the symbol of a militant
political programme.

But the language of a unique female mission was dangerously
ambiguous. The same words carried meanings which were not only
distinct but sometimes absolutely antagonistic to each other: Kate
was writing her tracts at the same time as evangelical women such as
Sarah Lewis were propounding their own views on women's 'regener-
ating' moral role, frequently expressed in terms nearly as apoca-
lyptic as those of the Communist Church. Nor were socialist writers
free from this anti-feminist interpretation of women's unique
function: the Reverend Smith, for all his principled stands on
female unionism, denied that women had any right to vote since their
influence was moral rather than political; (85) another writer in
the Communist press called 'Pause' celebrated women's wifely and
maternal mission in terms befitting any Victorian patriarch.

And with the decline of socialist feminism in the late 1840s, it
was Victorian patriarchalism which became dominant. Love, which the
Communists wished to see 'socialise our planet' was rhetorically
roped back into the bedroom and kitchen, and for both working-class
and middle-class women 'female influence' became a synonym for the
reality of social powerlessness. Ruskin took over where the
struggle between conservative ideologues and the feminists had left
off: 'A true wife, in her husband's house, is his servant; it is
in his heart that she is queen.' (86) The women of the radical
movements who had demanded power outside the cosy confines of the
male heart had fought hard against this developing orthodoxy. As
one feminist wrote to the 'New Moral World':

reformers dwell generally greatly on the influence of women over
society, when they should first explain to them that they have
no power ... if woman has influence over society, men have power
over it, and which is more respected and obeyed, the slave or the
tyrant?

Writers on the subject of women's maternal mission, she went on,
'appear to delight to consider women as inferior beings. We never
see long treatises on the duty of man.' (87)

With the collapse of the socialist movement in 1845 this radical
understanding of women's alienation lost its most important
platform. (88) The working-class politics which developed after
1850 did not begin to express these ideas again until the last
decades of the century, and then only among certain small groups
or individuals. Nor did the middle-class feminism of the second
half of the nineteenth century systematically challenge women's
social and class position in the way that women such as Kate had
done. The fading of the Owenite heretical imagination which had
envisaged workers' power and women's liberation as morally and politically inseparable had important consequences for the struggle
of working-class women: for them it meant not only the loss of
their tentative strategical base of the 1830s and 1840s, but also
the decline of a radical culture and language rich in the symbols
of emancipation. The language in which the doctrine of the female
Messiah had been expressed was not less subversive for its mysti-
cism, just as the first socialist movement was no less ideologically
combative because it drew some rhetorical weapons from religious
cults. The final word to Reverend Smith, who puts it well:

Reason and vision come all from one source.... The Socialist,
who preaches of community of goods, abolition of crime, of
punishment, of magistrates, and of marriage, is accounted equally
deranged as the followers of Joanna Southcotte (sic) ... it may
be as well for you to suspect that you may learn something from
them. (89)

NOTES

1 Southcott, Joanna, The Strange Effects of Faith, 1802. The
   following account of Southcott's life and writings is drawn from
   her own writings, as compiled in Alice Seymour's 'The Express:
   ... containing the Life and Divine Writings of the Late Joanna
   Southcott', London, 1909, and from the following secondary ma-
   terial: G.R.Balleine, 'Past Finding Out: the Tragic Story of
   Joanna Southcott and Her Successors', SPCK, London, 1956;
   J.Evans, 'Sketch of the various Denominations of the Christian
   World', 1841 edition; J.F.C.Harrison, 'Robert Owen and the
   Owenites in Britain and America, the Quest for the New Moral
   World', Routledge & Kegan Paul, London, 1969, pp.109-12;
   Charles A.Lane, 'Life and Bibliography of Joanna Southcott',
   1912; Mary S.Robertson, 'The True Story of Joanna Southcott',
   Ashford, Middsx, 1923; James Elishma Smith, 'The Coming Man',
   London, 1875; Robert Southey, 'Letters from England', ed.
   J.Simmons, London, 1951, Letter 70; E.P.Thompson, 'The Making
   of the English Working Class', Penguin, Harmondsworth, 1972,
   pp.420-6.
2 Balleine, op.cit., p.46.
3 Harrison, op.cit., p.110.
4 Seymour, op.cit., vol.1, p.52.
5 Balleine, op.cit., p.24.
6 Thompson, op.cit., p.423.
7 Balleine, op.cit., p.47.
8 Seymour, op.cit., vol.1, p.122.

9   Joanna Southcott, Letters to Jane Townley, 1804, p.55.
10 Seymour, op.cit., vol.1, p.122.
11 The debate with Satan is to be found in Seymour, vol.2, p.97,
    in Southey, and in 'A letter addressed to the Rev. T.P.Foley ...
    upon the subject of his sanctioning and supporting the Pre-
    tensions of Joanna Southcott ...', Anon., 1813.
12 Seymour, vol.1, p.65.
13 Ibid., vol.1, p.67.
14 Ibid., vol.1, p.228.
15 Balleine, op.cit., p.58.
16 Thompson, op.cit., p.428. Both Thompson and Harrison point to
    the penetration of Southcottianism into the Owenite movement,
    and locate it within the millennialist current of early radical
    politics. I found their arguments very helpful and illumi-
    nating, while finding myself disagreeing with some of their
    interpretations of the ideological significance of millennialist
    heresies (see p.130 of this article).
17 See Keith Thomas, Women and the Civil War Sects, 'Past and
    Present', no.19, for a fascinating account of this.
18 Sheila Rowbotham, 'Hidden from History', Pluto Press, London,
    1973, p.16.
19 See Thompson, op.cit., chapters 11 and 16, and Eric Hobsbawm,
    The Labour Sects, in 'Primitive Rebels', Manchester University
    Press, 1959, for two important discussions of religious enthusi-
    asm and radicalism of this period.
20 A valuable discussion of radicalism and plebeian religion is to
    be found in Eileen Yeo's 'Christianity and Chartist Culture'
    (MS in author's possession). I am grateful to her for letting
    me see this essay; to it and to her Robert Owen and Radical
    Culture in S.Pollard and J.Salt, eds, 'Robert Owen, Prophet of
    the Poor', Macmillan, London, 1971, as well as to our dis-
    cussions of Owenism, this essay owes much.
21 'Manchester Observer', 7 July 1819, quoted in K.A.Corfield, Some
    Social and Radical Organisations among Working-Class Women in
    Manchester and District, 1750-1820, University of Birmingham,
    B.A. Dissertation, unpublished, 1970.
22 Balleine, op.cit., pp.71,77,112. His accounts of Allman and
    Turner are drawn largely from Smith.
23 Ibid., pp.111,55.
24 Thompson, op.cit., p.879; Balleine, op.cit., p.112.
    Mrs Vaughan led an attack on Ward, according to Balleine.
25 The account of Smith given here is necessarily brief and omits
    much of the career of this extraordinary man. A useful, but
    biased, source on his life is the account written by his nephew,
    W.A.Smith, '"Shepherd" Smith the Universalist; the Story of a
    Mind', London, 1892; for his millennialism, see the excellent
    account in Harrison. John Saville's J.E.Smith and the Owenite
    Movement, 1833-34, in Pollard and Salt, op.cit., is very good on
    Smith's political work and writings. Smith's feminism has not
    been discussed, although Harrison does mention it. Smith's own
    writings are to be found in 'Isis', 1832, 'The Crisis', 1832-4,
    'The Pioneer', 1833-4, 'The Shepherd', 1834-8, 'New Moral
    World', 1834-45, and several books and tracts, some of which are
    referred to elsewhere in the article.

26 His 'The Coming Man' described the time he spent among the
    Southcottian sect led by John Wroe in Ashton, calling themselves
    the Christian Israelites. There is a hostile account of this
    sect in T.Fielden, 'An Exposition of the Fallacies and Absurdi-
    ties of that Deluded Church known as the Christian Israelites
    ...', 1851, in which one of their hymns is reproduced:
    Till now the woman ne'er became
    An helpmate for the man;
    Unless to help him to the tomb
    As she at first began.
    But now she helps the man to rise,
    As once she helped his fall;
    And now he owns that God was wise,
    And just and true in all.
27 There are innumerable accounts of Owen and the Owenite movement,
    few of which even mention the feminism of the movement. The
    best of these are Harrison, Pollard and Salt, and Thompson, pp.
    857-87. There is a very interesting examination of Owenite
    feminism in John Killham, 'Tennyson and the Princess: Re-
    flections of an Age', London, 1958, in which Saint-Simonian
    women are also discussed.
28 'Articles of Agreement for the formation of a Community on
    Principles of Mutual Co-operation, to be located within fifty
    miles of London', London, 1825, articles 8 and 9.
29 See, for example, 'The Co-Operative Magazine', May 1826 and
    February 1827; 'The British Co-Operator', April 1830; 'Poor
    Man's Guardian', 26 May 1832, 16 March 1833, 14 September 1833.
30 'The Crisis', 3 May 1834.
31 For an analysis of these changes and their impact on women
    workers, see in particular Sally Alexander, Women and the London
    Trades, 1830-50, in J.Mitchell and A.Oakley, eds, 'The Rights
    and Wrongs of Women', Penguin, Harmondsworth, 1976.
32 'The Pioneer', 12 April 1834.
33 'The Crisis', 1 March 1834.
34 'The Shepherd', 15 August 1835.
35 'The Crisis', 31 August 1833.
36 21 February 1835.
37 15 June 1833.
38 The story has been told by Richard Pankhurst, in his 'The Saint-
    Simonians, Mill and Carlyle', London, 1957.
39 Ibid., p.71.
40 'Poor Man's Guardian', 11 January 1834, 5 April 1834; 'True
    Sun', 11 April 1834.
41 'The Destructive', 4 January 1834. This newspaper also carried
    an account of one of these meetings where the Saint-Simonian
    lecturer announced that 'he had studied Gall and had phreno-
    logically studied many women's heads, whose organs, save that
    of combativeness ... were even more fully developed than those
    of men'. In an editorial of 2 November 1833, Henry Hetherington
    discussed their views on women and 'moral marriage' (they be-
    lieved in cohabitation) and growled: 'Why talk of making women
    rational until we have first made ourselves rational? or why
    talk of restoring them to their social rights, till we have
    first obtained our own?'

42   She was the common-law wife of Richard Carlile and editress of
     'Isis', which contained a number of feminist articles.
43   'St.Simonism in London by Fontana and Prati, Chief and Preacher
     of Saint-Simonism in London', London, 1834.
44   Reprinted in 'The Destructive', 2 November 1833.
45   'The Movement', no.5, p.40, 1843.
46   'London Social Reformer', 9 May 1840.
47   'New Moral World', 27 April 1839.
48   'Pioneer', 12 April 1834.
49   John Finch, 'Bible of the Reformation Reformed', I, xliv-xlv,
     quoted in Harrison, op.cit., p.125.
50   G.J.Holyoake, 'The Last Days of Emma Martin', 1851; Emma
     Martin, 'A Few Reasons for Renouncing Christianity and Pro-
     fessing and Disseminating Infidel Opinions', 1852?
51   Harrison, op.cit., p.135. Harrison comes to this evaluation at
     the conclusion of a long and very valuable discussion of Owenite
     millennialism to which I am heavily indebted, even while disa-
     greeing with some of its emphases.
52   J.G.Barmby, in 'The Promethean, or Communist Apostle', January
     1842.
53   'New Moral World', 6 April 1839.
54   'Dictionary of National Biography'. Information on the Barmbys
     and the Communist Church is scattered throughout contemporary
     and secondary sources for early English radicalism; no system-
     atic account has been written. My account is drawn from 'The
     New Moral World'; 'The Educational Circular and Communist
     Apostle', 1842; 'New Tracts for the Times', 1843; 'The Apostle
     and Chronicle of the Communist Church', 1848; contemporary
     commentators such as G.J.Holyoake, 'The History of Co-Operation
     in England: its Literature and its Advocates', 2 vols, London,
     1880, and W.H.G.Armytage's The Journalistic Activities of
     J.Goodwyn Barmby between 1841 and 1848, 'Notes and Queries',
     CCl, 1956.
55   See, for example, 'New Moral World', 25 July, 15 August, 24 Oc-
     tober, 1840.
56   'New Moral World', 5 September 1840. According to Barmby,
     Tristan gave him a gift of two seals, 'the one emblematical of
     her political, the other, of her religious opinions. The po-
     litical seal is of a triangular form, with the word "Unity" in
     the middle, and the words, "Gods", "Liberty", and "Franchise" on
     the three sides. In the centre of the religious seal is "Gods";
     amid the triangle are the words "Father", "Mother", "Embryo"'.
57   'New Moral World', 25 April 1840.
58   'The Promethean or Communist Apostle', February 1842.
59   Armytage, op.cit.
60   'New Moral World', 28 August 1841.
61   George Bird, who also lectured on medicine and Communism - a pet
     theme of Barmby's. 'New Moral World', 4 September 1841.
62   'New Moral World', 8 February 1840.
63   'The Working Bee' at the Community Press, Manea Fen, Cambridge-
     shire, 14 September 1839.
64   See the account of the debate between Owen and John Brindley in
     'What is Socialism?', Bristol, 1841, and many similar accounts
     throughout the 'New Moral World'.

65 Joseph Barker, 'The Overthrow of Infidel Socialism', London, 1840.
66 'Fraser's Magazine', Women and the Social System, June 1840.
67 'Is Marriage Worth Perpetuating', London City Mission, 1840.
68 Frost, op.cit., pp.16-20.
69 Barker, op.cit.; Edward Hancock, 'Robert Owen's Community System ... and the horrid Doings of the St.Simonians, in Beaumont Square, ... a new Sect from France', Letter Third, London, 1837.
70 'New Moral World', 26 June 1841.
71 Ibid., 28 January 1843.
72 Sarah Lewis, 'Woman's Mission', London, seventh edition, 1842, p.54.
73 Charlotte Elizabeth Tonna, 'The Wrongs of Woman', 1843, p.4. But if the evangelicals could draw modern lessons from the scriptures, so could other women:

> the blame lieth upon the woman, without discerning that Adam was as easy to fall ... But see, how the blame was cast. These things men do not discern; therefore they go on, as Adam began, to cast blame upon the woman.

Thus Joanna Southcott. Here is 'Syrtis', the Socialist feminist, on the same theme:

> Had the account of 'the Fall' been penned by a woman, we should have had a very different version of it. Eve's great folly would then have been represented to consist in allowing her spouse to partake of the knowledge which was to make them as gods. Had she succeeded in concealing the extent of the power she possessed, as many modern ladies have done, she might have ruled by her reason, instead of becoming the slave of man's passions, and 'multiplying her sorrows and her conception'.

74 'The Christian Lady's Magazine', vol.13, 1840, pp.378-80.
75 1 May 1841.
76 'The Movement', vol.2, 1844, p.64.
77 Catherine Isabella Barmby, Invocation, 'Educational Circular', 1841, p.27.
78 'New Moral World', 17 July 1841.
79 'Educational Circular', no.1, 1841, p.6.
80 Frost, op.cit., p.79.
81 'Tracts for the Times', February 1842.
82 'New Moral World', 17 July 1841.
83 'New Tracts for the Times', vol.1, no.3, 1843.
84 'Apostle and Chronicle of the Communist Church', 1848.
85 'The Shepherd', 21 February 1835.
86 The Crown of Wild Olive, in 'The Works of John Ruskin', xviii, p.496, quoted in F.Basch, 'Relative Creatures', 1975, p.6.
87 'New Moral World', 4 January 1843.
88 The Socialist movement suffered a terrible blow with the collapse of their official community at Queenswood in 1845, and soon faded out as an organised presence on the radical scene. The Communist Church carried on for some time: in 1847 it established a Poplar branch and in 1848 Barmby was the Church's delegate to revolutionary circles in Paris. Kate turns up in left-wing literary circles in the same period. Goodwyn later

became a Unitarian minister in Wakefield, where he seems to have remained politically active until his death in 1881; Kate's later career I have not been able to trace.

89   'The Crisis', 31 August 1833.

Index